Cambridge Elements

Elements in Corporate Governance
edited by
Thomas Clarke
UTS Business School, University of Technology Sydney

REGULATING EU SUSTAINABILITY REPORTING

Learning from Failure and Success

David Monciardini
University of Turin

Shaftesbury Road, Cambridge CB2 8EA, United Kingdom

One Liberty Plaza, 20th Floor, New York, NY 10006, USA

477 Williamstown Road, Port Melbourne, VIC 3207, Australia

314–321, 3rd Floor, Plot 3, Splendor Forum, Jasola District Centre, New Delhi – 110025, India

103 Penang Road, #05–06/07, Visioncrest Commercial, Singapore 238467

Cambridge University Press is part of Cambridge University Press & Assessment, a department of the University of Cambridge.

We share the University's mission to contribute to society through the pursuit of education, learning and research at the highest international levels of excellence.

www.cambridge.org
Information on this title: www.cambridge.org/9781009737128

DOI: 10.1017/9781009737104

© David Monciardini 2025

This publication is in copyright. Subject to statutory exception and to the provisions of relevant collective licensing agreements, no reproduction of any part may take place without the written permission of Cambridge University Press & Assessment.

When citing this work, please include a reference to the DOI 10.1017/9781009737104

First published 2025

A catalogue record for this publication is available from the British Library

ISBN 978-1-009-73712-8 Hardback
ISBN 978-1-009-73708-1 Paperback
ISSN 2515-7175 (online)
ISSN 2515-7167 (print)

Cambridge University Press & Assessment has no responsibility for the persistence or accuracy of URLs for external or third-party internet websites referred to in this publication and does not guarantee that any content on such websites is, or will remain, accurate or appropriate.

For EU product safety concerns, contact us at Calle de José Abascal, 56, 1°, 28003 Madrid, Spain, or email eugpsr@cambridge.org

Regulating EU Sustainability Reporting

Learning from Failure and Success

Elements in Corporate Governance

DOI: 10.1017/9781009737104
First published online: September 2025

David Monciardini
University of Turin

Author for correspondence: David Monciardini, david.monciardini@unito.it

Abstract: Deterioration of socio-ecological systems requires deep changes in business regulation, including accounting rules. However, policymakers and stakeholders have recursively failed to deliver on mandatory sustainability reporting. Over the last decade, things have rapidly changed. Particularly in the EU, we are witnessing the standardisation and harmonisation of sustainability reporting. This Element questions what explains changes in sustainability reporting regulation and what one can learn from the past. It suggests that there is a structural fallacy in the design of the regulation of accounting for sustainability, which needs to be addressed to avoid another failure. The Element concludes by setting out a bold blueprint for rethinking reporting regulation based on a series of paradigmatic changes.

Keywords: sustainability reporting, EU regulation, corporate governance, accounting, regulatory capture

© David Monciardini 2025

ISBNs: 9781009737128 (HB), 9781009737081 (PB), 9781009737104 (OC)
ISSNs: 2515-7175 (online), 2515-7167 (print)

Contents

1	Introduction	1
2	Unpacking the Sustainability Reporting Conundrum	5
3	History of Sustainability Reporting	22
4	Putting the Pieces Together: What Explains Changes?	32
5	Learning from Failure and Success: Proposals for a Paradigmatic Change	44
	List of Abbreviations	61
	References	62

The lack of explicit rules has contributed to a situation where different stakeholders, including regulatory authorities, investors, financial analysts and the public in general may consider the environmental information disclosed by companies to be either inadequate or unreliable. ... In the absence of harmonised authoritative guidelines in relation to environmental issues and financial reporting, comparability between companies becomes difficult. (*European Commission Recommendation, 4th and 5th Recitals of the Preamble, 2001*)

... the pace of progress towards more transparent disclosure practices remains slow, and a majority of users (including in particular investors, NGOs and other civil society organisations) consider the current level of transparency in this field as unable to meet their needs. Specific issues have been highlighted with regard to both quantity and quality of information available. (*European Commission, Impact Assessment, Proposal for Non-financial Reporting Directive, 2013*)

Unfortunately, TV footage of raging bushfires in Australia, melting icebergs in Antarctica, freak weather in general, have become commonplace. ... This will require companies to increase disclosure on their sustainable activities, and give adequate reliable information on sustainability risks and opportunities. ... The many overlapping international reporting standards and set-ups confuse companies and investors. (*European Commission, Executive Vice-President Dombrovskis, 2020*)

1 Introduction

Political and business leaders find themselves in a complex multi-crises (or permacrisis) scenario and need to retool and scale up their twentieth-century decision-making and risk assessment tools to face the great socio-ecological challenges ahead (Brand-Correa et al., 2022; Brown et al., 2024). It is widely shared that our present form of extractive and predatory capitalism (Lazonick and Shin, 2019) is the cause of intensifying climate change, species extinction, habitat destruction, and chemical pollution alongside increased levels of inequality (IPCC, 2023; EEA, 2024). In light of these circumstances, there is a growing awareness of the need for businesses to align themselves with these changing social and environmental sustainability dynamics. Developing appropriate policies and regulation to provide an enabling infrastructure for this transition has therefore become crucial (Kourula et al., 2019; Hoffman, 2023). Accounting rules, according to which companies draw up their corporate reports, are one of the central pieces of this rapidly changing regulatory jigsaw (Sjåfjell and Bruner, 2019; Monciardini et al., 2020; Hahn et al., 2023; Barker and Mayer, 2024; Vollmer, 2024).

There is already a burgeoning literature dedicated to corporate sustainability reporting (hereafter SR), to which I direct for a more detailed and comprehensive overview of this field of research (Laine et al., 2022; De Villers et al., 2022; Barker and Mayer, 2023; Hummel and Jobst, 2024; Magnan and Michelon, 2024; Vollmer, 2024). This is driven by a remarkable increase in both the number of SR being issued and the number of private and public regulatory initiatives (Magnan and Michelon, 2024; IFAG, 2025). However, SR regulation research remains under-theorised (Barker and Mayer, 2023) and polarised between utopic dreams of corporate reporting inducing strong societal changes and dismal considerations about the lack of a real breakthrough (Cho et al., 2015b). The regulatory field is also characterised by fragmentation and pre-defined conceptual divides (e.g. financial or non-financial; narrative or quantitative disclosure; single or double materiality; social or environmental information; national legislation or global harmonisation) that risk creating confusion and polarisation. As we shall see throughout this work, SR is a contested and ambiguous concept. As a working definition, for the scope of this study, SR refers to "a range of techniques, tools and practices that are used in the measurement, planning, control and accountability of organisations with regard to environmental, social and economic issues" (Laine et al., 2022: 2). Here, I adopt the term SR as an 'umbrella terminology' for a broad range of corporate reporting practices (CSR reports, ESG disclosure, etc.) that have their own definitions and rationales but can be seen as part of a common history. Regulation is broadly defined as "all forms of formal and informal rule pertaining to some collective (nation, groups, sectors) where those rules are either binding to the members of that collective or at least significantly constrain their behaviour. This involves both public and private (self-)regulation..." (Overbeek et al., 2007: 5). The contribution of this study builds on a methodology defined by Pierre Bourdieu as 'double historicisation' (see Section 2.5). This can be defined as a historicisation of the object of the study, the regulation of SR in Europe, but also a historicisation of the 'tradition', the conventional construction of the object (Bourdieu, 1984 and 1996; Madsen, 2006). In line with this idea, the work situates SR regulation using a historical perspective, identifying various regulatory waves or layers relating to changes in SR frameworking and conceptualisation. I suggest that using this approach can help to advance a deeper theorisation of SR, overcoming the conceptual fragmentation and confusion that characterises the current regulatory debate.

The research is dedicated to explain changes in the regulation of SR in Europe over an extensive period of time, from the 1970s to date (May 2025). It is worth looking at the European context because this has been the area of the world that has seen greater initiatives in this regulatory field. While the history of SR in Europe has been far from linear and straightforward, this is rarely acknowledged because studies tend to only focus on the latest developments, overlooking important lessons from the past. As we shall see in Section 3, in the 1970s there was a strong debate demanding to reform accounting laws. Then it disappeared in the 1980s. The 1990s mark the return of SR but separate from accounting laws, only based on voluntary standards such as the GRI and EMAS. In the 2000s we had new demands for mandatory reports that failed to deliver changes in accounting laws, resulting in the development of ever more voluntary standards such as CDP and the Global Compact. Lastly, changes in EU accounting laws succeeded to be adopted in the 2010s and in the last decade we have witnessed an 'explosion' of SR regulation. However, rather than a radical change in existing EU financial reporting rules, SR has emerged as a separate set of legislative initiatives. Thus, this study aims at explaining this cyclical development, questioning in particular:

> *What explains recursive SR regulatory failures and why SR has emerged as separate from the regulation of financial accounting?*

In contrast to a conventional depoliticised and decontextualised view of accounting standards, I draw on sociological studies of accounting to underline the mutually constitutive nature of accounting, organising, and economising (Hopwood, 1983 and 2007; Miller and Power, 2013). Social theorists such as Weber and Sombart and historians have indeed shown that accounting has had a remarkable impact on the construction of modern capitalism (Carruthers and Espeland, 2012). Deploying a 'double historicisation' research methodology, the specific contribution of this work has been to look at the history of SR in the context of contemporary developments in financial accounting regulation and broader changes in value creation regimes. This integrated approach helps in understanding the cyclical development of SR regulation and recursive regulatory failures as part of the struggles for changing the institutionalised field of accounting.

In this Element, I argue that there is a structural fallacy in the design of accounting rules for sustainability. Since the 1980s, European financial accounting has been increasingly seen as merely technical, monolithic, and stable representations of micro-level organisational practices, detached from large economic, societal, and ecological questions. Thus, social and environmental matters are framed as externalities, extraneous, and marginalised in relation to current financial accounting rules. The global financial crisis started in 2008, and the role played by accounting rules – that is, fair value measurement – in exacerbating its effects on economies powerfully demonstrated the close relationship between accounting rules and economic ordering (e.g. Plantin et al., 2008; Miller and Power, 2013). Before in the US and UK and from the 1990s and 2000s also in Continental Europe, governments proceeded towards a global integration and deregulation of financial markets to sustain economic growth (Strange, 1996; Jessop 1992 and 2007; Aglietta and Reberioux 2005; Epstein, 2005). This has been based on the creation of common financial accounting rules, focusing only on financially material information (Hopwood, 1994; Botzem and Quack, 2005). Inspired by the Anglo-Saxon accounting tradition, the European harmonisation and global diffusion of accounting standards narrowly focused on the needs of capital providers played a key role in the emergence of a "money concept of corporate control" (Lazonick & Shin, 2019). By the same token, I argue that the need to narrowly focus on financial information explains parallel failures to develop strong SR regulation. Thus, financialised accounting and value capture go hand in hand with the problems of social and environmental (un)sustainability. In this historical perspective, I understand current attempts to harmonise and standardise SR regulation that followed the 2008 global financial crisis as an attempt to respond to the need to find accounting standards that reflect value creation and valuation in the Anthropocene. Current EU accounting standards, and their underlying notions of value, do not fit for purpose and can even increase the risk of socio-economic and ecological unsustainability.

The purpose of this work is not only to summarise the wealth of extant analyses of SR regulation but to try to find a preliminary synthesis, a new basis on which it is possible to think about a variety of issues as an emergent research and policy agenda. In particular, my aim has been to question systemic issues and deep structures that appear to impose important constraints on the effective regulation of corporate reporting. The remainder of this Element is organised as follows. The next section offers a critical overview of current EU policy, focusing on the Corporate Sustainability Reporting Directive (hereafter CSRD), the creation of the European Standards for Sustainability Reporting (hereafter ESRS), and the contested Omnibus proposal aimed at streamlining various SR requirements. The section briefly outlines the core argument of the Element: there is a structural fallacy in the design of EU accounting rules for sustainability that explains recursive regulatory failures. Section 3 provides an overview of the historical development of SR regulation in the European context. Covering the period from the 1970s to date, the section identifies three main waves through which SR has emerged. Each wave started with high hopes for fundamental changes but resulted in regulatory failure. Section 4 attempts to explain recursive regulatory failures by considering parallel developments in the history of financial reporting harmonisation and standardisation. I make the argument that SR can be better understood as a part of ongoing struggles to address the shortcomings of the financial accounting paradigm. Section 5 concludes by outlining a series of paradigmatic changes in the EU public debate on mandatory SR.

2 Unpacking the Sustainability Reporting Conundrum

2.1 An Overview of Current EU Policy

As discussed in the following sections, attempts to regulate SR in Europe have a long history that goes back, at least, to the 1970s (Mathews, 1997; Owen, 2008; Buhr et al., 2014; Magnan and Michelon, 2024). Under the first von der Leyen Commission, the debate about SR regulation has become particularly intense. As part of the European Green Deal (European Commission, 2019b), on 21 April 2021, the European Commission issued a legislative proposal aimed at fundamentally changing and strengthening the nature and extent of SR in the EU. In January 2023, this regulatory process culminated in the entry into force of the Corporate Sustainability Reporting Directive (CSRD), followed by the adoption of the European Sustainability Reporting Standards (ESRS), in July 2023 (Figure 1).

As illustrated by Figure 1, over the period of 2018–2025, European institutions have also promoted and adopted other groundbreaking corporate accountability legislation (for an overview see Hummel and Jobst, 2024). The EU developed a classification system established to clarify which economic activities are environmentally sustainable, the Taxonomy for Sustainable Activities (hereafter EU Taxonomy). It was published in the Official Journal of the European Union in June 2020. The Sustainable Finance Disclosure Regulation (hereafter SFDR) came into force on 10 March 2021. It applies to all financial market participants, which are required to disclose how they consider sustainability risks and adverse sustainability impacts in their investment processes and products. The Corporate Sustainability Due Diligence Directive (hereafter CSDDD) requires due diligence for companies to prevent adverse human rights and environmental impacts in the company's own operations and across their value chains. It was proposed in February 2022 and adopted by the Council of the European Union only on 24 May 2024. Thus, the EU sustainability reporting regulation (CSRD/ESRS) is only one important piece of a major tectonic shift in the EU legislation (see Sjåfjell and Bruner, 2019; Sjåfjell, 2024). However, opposition to this wave of EU corporate sustainability laws has also grown stronger, aimed at blocking or watering down the reform process. Finally, in February 2025, von der Leyen proposed to roll back all three EU corporate sustainability flagship initiatives – the EU Taxonomy, CSRD, and CSDDD – a legislative package known as the Omnibus I and II regulation. This contested U-turn was motivated by the need to reduce the regulatory burden for companies.

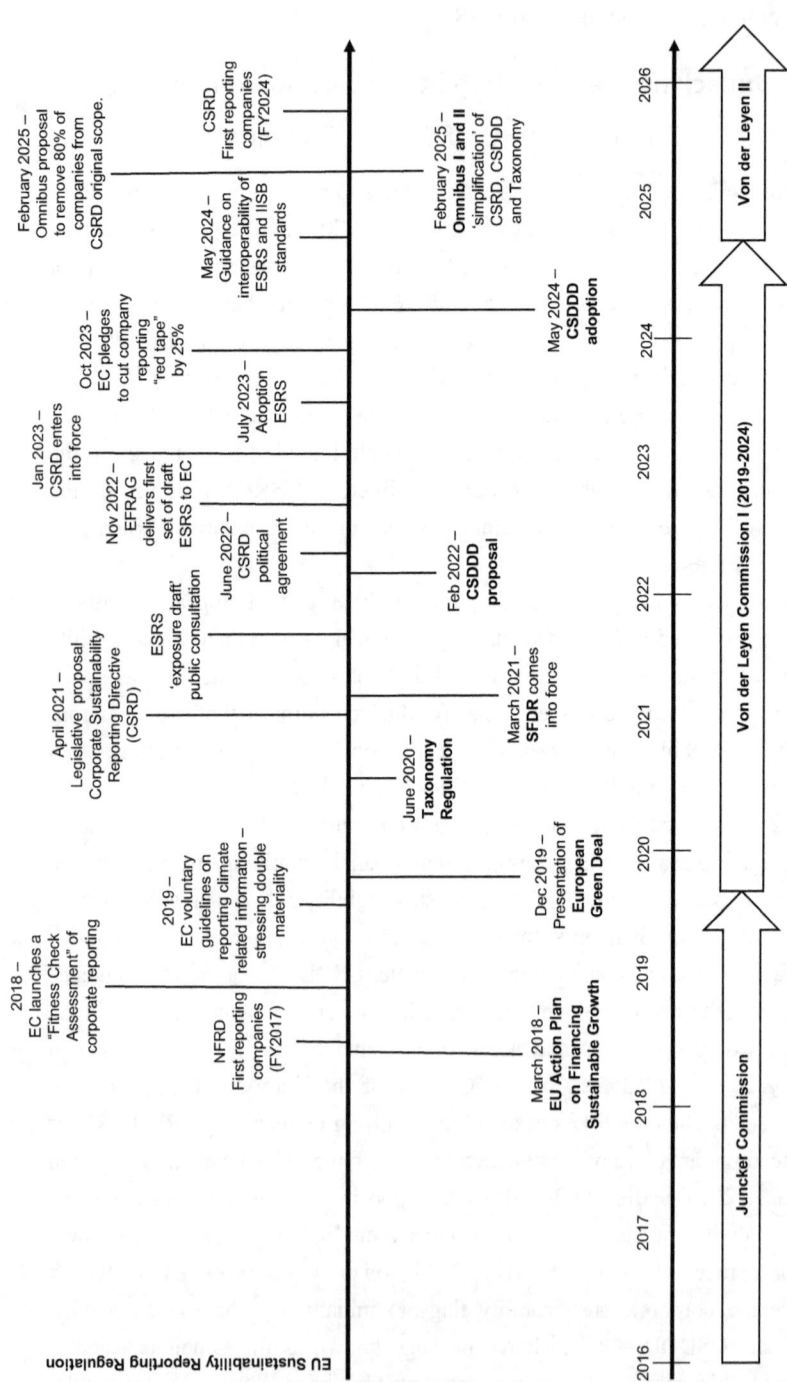

Figure 1 Timeline of the EU regulation of corporate sustainability reporting (2018–2025)

The following pages will set out by briefly introducing the main features of the CSRD legislation, its implementation through the ESRS, considering both strengths and shortcomings, and recent developments related to the 2025 Omnibus I and II packages.

2.1.1 The Corporate Sustainability Reporting Directive

The CSRD entered into force on 5th January 2023 and companies started to apply the new rules for the first time in the 2024 financial year, with reports published in 2025. It was adopted to address some of the weaknesses of the pre-existing 2014 European Directive on Non-Financial Reporting (NFRD), repeatedly criticised for deficiencies regarding comparability, consistency, and reliability of the information and the limited number of companies in scope (La Torre et al., 2018; Monciardini et al., 2020; European Commission, 2021). Compared to the NFRD, the CSRD represented a 'sea change' in many aspects, including:

- an extension of the *companies in scope* to approximately 50,000 European companies, compared to previous 11,700 (only unlisted SMEs and micro-enterprises are excluded and subsidiaries of non-EU companies that have a net turnover lower than EUR 150 million in the EU);
- an extension of the reporting requirements for a company's *value chain*;
- further specifications of the *double materiality* concept and *reporting contents*;
- a rejection of the term '*non-financial*' as inaccurate and misleading, recognising that sustainability-related information has financial relevance;
- requirements for the *integration of sustainability information* in the management report (a separate SR is no longer possible);
- *limited assurance* (audit) on the company's SR carried out by the statutory auditors, foreseeing the possibility of a transition to reasonable assurance by October 2028;
- *digital tagging* of the information reported to make them machine readable and enable their entry into a European Single Access Point (ESAP), reducing costs of data collection and increase its comparability and use by stakeholders;

The CSRD introduces a useful distinction between the "ultimate beneficiaries" of better SR and its "primary groups of users" (para 9). The former include savers "who want to invest sustainably", "trade unions and workers' representatives who would be adequately informed and therefore able to better engage in social dialogue", and "all citizens would benefit from a stable, sustainable and inclusive economic system". According to the directive, the empowerment of two primary groups of users of SR information is the key to "realise such benefits". The first group consists of investors who want to better understand risks and opportunities of their investments. The second group consists of civil society actors, "which wish to better hold undertakings to account for their impacts on people and the environment". Other groups of stakeholders are also cited as potential users of SR, in particular costumes, policy makers and environmental agencies.

An important feature of the CSRD is that SR becomes more than just a communication exercise. Issuers are required to explain the relevance of sustainability-related factors to their operating model and forward-looking business strategy. This includes "implementing actions and related financial and investment plans, to ensure that its business model and strategy are compatible with the transition to a sustainable economy and with the limiting of global warming to 1,5 °C in line with the Paris Agreement" (Article 29a). Progress has to be measured against "time-bound targets related to sustainability information" (Article 19a). The directive also requires the disclosure of information about the role of the administrative, management, and supervisory bodies with regard to sustainability matters, and of their expertise and skills in relation to fulfilling that role. Relatedly, companies are required to disclose whether they have adopted incentive schemes linked to sustainability objectives. Another potentially very significant change concerns the integration of SR into the annual report that contributes to underlining the close link between the sustainability and business strategy of the firm. Over time, this integration is likely to trigger internal strategic discussions and knowledge transfer among different business functions and across the company's value chain.

The CSRD was adopted with a phased-in application, starting in 2025, when the 11,000 companies already subject to the NFRD were required to issue the first ESRS-compliant reports, and gradually extending its application to include approximately 50,000 companies by 2028. Notably, listed SMEs were given a possibility of voluntary opt-out until 2028, reporting according to separate, proportionate standards. The CSRD explains the rationale for this wide scope: "In view of the growth of users' needs for sustainability information, additional categories of undertakings should be required to report sustainability information. It is therefore appropriate to require all large undertakings and all undertakings, except micro undertakings, whose securities are admitted to trading on a regulated market in the Union to report sustainability information" (para 17).

To ensure the quality of reporting, the information disclosed should be "relevant, comparable, and reliable" (para 2). The CSRD describes this quality improvement as a "prerequisite" for meeting the overarching transformational policy objectives of the 2019 European Green Deal and the 2018 'Action Plan:

Financing Sustainable Growth' (para 1 and 2). Quality is achieved through the implementation of three key processes: the double materiality assessment (DMA), corporate sustainability due diligence (DD), and external assurance.

Double Materiality Assessment

Materiality is a key reporting principle aimed at guiding companies in assessing whether an information is relevant and needs to be disclosed (Cooper and Michelon, 2022). The NFRD already required to report both on the impacts of the activities of the undertaking on people and the environment and on how sustainability matters affect the undertaking. However, the CSRD underlines that this approach is "often not well understood or applied" (para 29). Building on the 2019 Commission's 'Guidelines on reporting climate-related information', the CSRD made this requirement more explicit, referring to it as "the double materiality perspective, in which the risks to the undertaking and the impacts of the undertaking each represent one materiality perspective" (para 37). The CSRD clarifies that issuers should disclose information that is material from both perspectives and information that is material from only one perspective (para 29).

Corporate sustainability due diligence

Due diligence (DD) was a key concept already in the 2013 NFRD (cited only two times) but its importance increases with the CSRD (cited eighteen times). Thus, the CSRD states that "the due diligence disclosure requirements should be specified in greater detail than" in the NFRD. In line with the UN Guiding Principles on Business and Human Rights (hereafter the UNGPs), the CSRD defines due diligence as "the process that undertakings carry out to identify, monitor, prevent, mitigate, remediate or bring an end to the principal actual and potential adverse impacts connected with their activities and identifies how undertakings address those adverse impacts". The directive stresses that "the due diligence process concerns the whole value chain of the undertaking". In particular, under the CSRD, companies are required to disclose (i) information about the DD process implementation, (ii) information about the principal actual or potential adverse impacts identified, and (iii) any actions taken to prevent, mitigate, remediate, or bring an end to actual or potential adverse impacts, and the result of such actions. It is important to stress that, in parallel with the CSRD initiative, in 2020, the European Commissioner for Justice, Didier Reynders, announced the introduction of rules for mandatory due diligence in relation to corporate sustainability: the CSDDD. The CSRD was designed to take into account the complementary CSDDD legislative developments. As noted by Shift in its guidance on CSRD implementation (2023), company resources spent on reporting are an investment in effective due diligence – and vice versa.

External assurance

One of the major shortcomings of the NFRD was the lack of external audit. It simply required statutory auditors or audit firms to check that a so-called 'nonfinancial information' statement or separate SR had been provided. It was not required to verify the information. Instead, to ensure that the information is reliable, the CSRD required the information disclosed to be externally audited "to meet the needs of the intended users of such information" (para 60). Thus, drawing on the assurance profession's distinction between limited and reasonable assurance engagements, under the CSRD, the information disclosed is subject to *limited assurance*. This is a simpler form of assurance, based on fewer tests than for a reasonable assurance. The main goal is to foster EU-wide consistency in establishing a new practice of SR assurance. On the basis of this process, the auditor expresses a conclusion in a negative form (e.g. 'no matter has been identified to conclude that the subject matter is materially misstated). However, the CSRD foresees a progressive shift towards more stringent and comprehensive reasonable auditing.

2.1.2 The European Standards for Sustainability Reporting

The European Commission has delegated the development of sustainability reporting standards to the European Financial Reporting Advisory Group (EFRAG), leading to the creation of the ESRS. It is worth briefly elaborating on the expertise and independence of this privately run and funded body, created in 2002 (Haller, 2002; Chiapello and Medjad, 2009; Giner and Luque-Vílchez, 2022; Mähönen and Palea, 2024).

EFRAG was created following the EU decision to adopt the International Financial Reporting Standards (IFRS) for the consolidated financial statements of all companies whose securities trade in a regulated market. This is a set of financial accounting standards elaborated by a private standard-setter based in London, the International Accounting Standards Board (IASB), which itself is controlled by the private IFRS Foundation. EFRAG serves as a bridge between the Commission, as a lawmaker, and the IASB, as a private standard-setter (Haller, 2002; Chiapello and Medjad, 2009). It was set up because, in the words of the Commission itself, "it is not possible politically, nor legally, to delegate accounting standard setting unconditionally and irrevocably to a private organisation [IASB] over which the EU has no influence" (in Chiapello and Medjad, 2009: 454). Thus,

EFRAG works very closely with the IASB/IFRS Foundation and it is tasked to advise the Commission on the IFRS adoption, proactively influence the IASB's standard-setting process, and check new IFRS drafts and standards for their compliance with European rules. Traditionally, its experience and mindset have been all about financial rather than sustainability reporting (Giner and Luque-Vílchez, 2022). Moreover, Mähönen and Palea (2024: 19) highlight that EFRAG receives "consistent contribution from accounting and business organizations, also in kind of staff secondment from accounting and business firms". EFRAG's Board is dominated by accounting professionals, listed companies, and financial institutions, such as banks and insurance companies. Only in November 2022, EFRAG set up the Sustainability Reporting Board (SRB), supported by a Technical Expert Group (TEG), to specifically advise on the development of ESRS, in accordance with the CSRD. The Chair of EFRAG SRB is appointed by the Commission and some members of the new Board represent civil society organisations and trade unions. However, the majority of EFRAG SRB's members are still accounting professionals, business associations, and financial institutions.

The draft standards proposed by EFRAG in June 2023 underwent significant changes required by the Commission. Specifically, the European Commission made three major modifications to the draft ESRS: phasing-in certain reporting requirements for companies with less than 750 employees (Scope 3 emissions and biodiversity-related topics), making all reporting requirements of the topical standards subject to the outcome of the double materiality assessment (except some ESRS 2 requirements), and converting some of the mandatory reporting requirements into voluntary. The ESRS was formally adopted by the European Commission in July 2023 and entered into the EU legal framework in October 2023.

Overall, the ESRS introduces more stringent, structured, and complex standards for SR, with the aim to increase the accuracy, reliability, and comparability of the information. The scale and implications of this innovation are unprecedented in the history of SR, traditionally left to the discretion of corporate management. Figure 2 provides an overview of the ESRS.

ESRS require companies to disclose material information regarding their sustainability impacts, risks, and opportunities (IROs), in accordance with applicable topical ESRS. As illustrated in Figure 2, the disclosure requirements are organised in cross-cutting (or 'general') standards (ESRS 1 and 2) and topical standards, which address a number of sustainability matters in three overarching reporting areas: Environment (ESRS E), Social (ESRS S), and Governance (ESRS G). Each reporting area is articulated into specific sustainability matters. If a specific sustainability matter is assessed as material (i.e. based on double materiality) by the company, it needs to disclose information

ESRS Standards

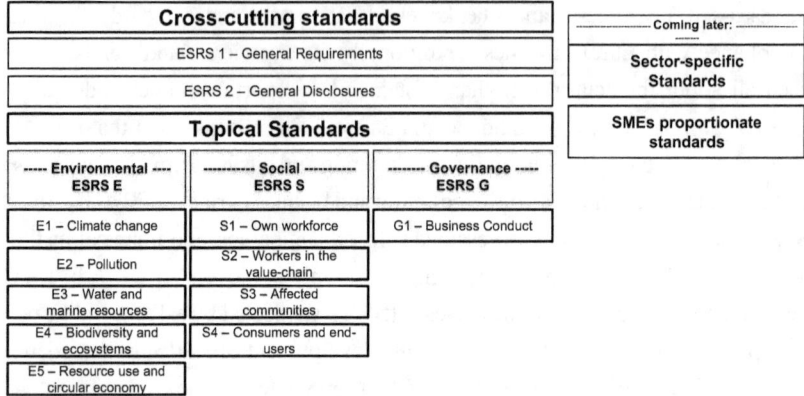

Figure 2 An overview of the European Sustainability Reporting Standards (ESRS)

according to the topical standard for that matter. ESRS include the development of ESRS LSME (for Listed SMEs) and ESRS VSME (Voluntary Standard for SMEs) to provide proportionate reporting requirements for smaller businesses. They also include the future development of sector-specific standards that were also meant to provide additional guidance.

As mentioned, the adoption of the CSRD/ESRS has represented a step change in the history of European SR regulation. The EU approach encourages companies to become more aware of the links between their commercial strategy and business model and their sustainability strategy. The assessment of the *impacts, risks, and opportunities* (i.e. IROs) that are material for their business encourages them to think strategically about their medium- to long-term resilience. It is crucial to underline that companies are required to report not only on their sustainability *policies* but also on how they translate them into *actions* (supported by adequate resources), to reach measurable, time-bound *targets* (i.e. PATs). This comprehensive data collection exercise requires companies to take, often for the first time, a more holistic view at the resilience of their own operations. This entails a fruitful dialogue within the company, across all key departments (e.g. the executive committee, finance and control, technology/IT, legal and tax compliance, operations and procurement).

Preliminary analyses of corporate reports issued in 2023 and 2024 according to ESRS show efforts to integrate SR information in the strategic development of firms (PwC, 2024; WAE and HEC, 2025). According to a large survey of over a thousand of companies in twenty-six countries (WAE and HEC, 2025), 54 per cent of firms are somewhat satisfied with the CSRD and 7 per cent very satisfied. Similar results emerge also as for SMEs (53%), which are often said to find compliance more challenging. Another research confirms that around three-quarters of companies give more weight to sustainability in business decisions. Crucially, it reveals that most companies are approaching CSRD implementation as a broad cross-functional effort, far beyond sustainability (PwC, 2024). Overall, preliminary research confirms that companies see multiple business benefits flowing from SR under the CSRD, including better risk management and mitigation, environmental performance, and improved stakeholder relations (PwC, 2024; WAE and HEC, 2025).

Lastly, the financial quantification of sustainability-related risks and opportunities is likely to strengthen the analytical basis used by companies, resulting in an enhancement of the quality of SR. As an example, in line with the CSRD, companies must report on their transition plan for climate change mitigation (ESRS E1). The objective is to ensure that their strategy and business model are compatible with the Paris Agreement and the EU's commitment to achieve climate neutrality by 2050. This includes the elaboration of an adequate action plan in relation to climate change and targets (E1-3).

However, the design and implementation of ESRS is also fraught with ambiguities and shortcomings. The main ones concern:

- the *excessive complexity of ESRS and lack of guidance*, seen by companies as unnecessarily costly and time-consuming (WAE and HEC, 2025). The first draft published by EFRAG in November 2022 included 136 disclosure requirements, then reduced to 84; and 2,161 quantitative and qualitative datapoints reduced to 1,144 in the final ESRS. This scared companies and transformed the original ambition of the CSRD in a tiresome compliance exercise. The risk is that SR comes to be perceived as "a great waste of time" and resources (Leinaweaver, 2015) – a 'tick-the-box', merely symbolic exercise (Edelman, 2016; Monciardini et al., 2021).
- shortcomings in the *legislative and standard-setting process* that led to the development of ESRS. EFRAG worked under a very tight deadline, lacking time and motivation, adequate resources and competences to deliver on such a delicate and challenging task. Insiders flagged issues around EFRAG's lack of sustainability expertise, lack of funding, and governance issues (Verney and Holmstedt Pell, 2023). The standard-setting process has been hastened and companies had too little time to adjust to this regulatory step change. A corporate representative, Ulrike Sapiro, Chief Sustainability Officer at Henkel (2025), expressed it vividly:

> We were still figuring out how to do it while the ink was not even dried on the legislative text. The guidance came in week by week. We looked constantly

over our shoulders, wondering: are we doing it the right way? ... It was a lot of flying the plane while you were still building it, literally. Which is not the ideal when it is about your annual report to the financial markets. So the stakes were quite high.

- the inclusion of SR into the annual report has been introduced *without a comprehensive reform of the EU accounting governance and standards*. This is particularly relevant because companies are now issuing the annual report according to two very different standards: part of the report according to IASB/IFRS, which adopt a very investor-driven ('single materiality') approach, and another part according to ESRS, which adopt a stakeholder-driven and double materiality approach. Sustainability data has simply been included into the annual report as an add-on, without explaining how issuers should enhance connectivity with financial information. This shortcoming is generating extremely long annual reports (i.e. hundreds of pages) that users find difficult to navigate (PwC, 2024; WAE and HEC, 2025).
- *ambiguity in the relationship between the ESRS and other SR standards*. First, it is unclear whether the relationship between the ESRS and other reporting standards can be defined as competing, converging, or complementary. This concerns the Global Reporting Initiative, the SR standard most widely adopted worldwide, as well as the new IFRS Sustainability Disclosure Standards (hereafter IFSR S) by the IFRS Foundation. In 2021–2022 the IFRS Foundation decided to establish a second standard-setting board, the International Sustainability Standards Board (ISSB), focused on SR (De Villiers et al., 2024; Giner and Luque-Vílchez, 2022). However, the latter differs in many fundamental aspects from the EU legislation (Baboukardos et al., 2023; Stolowy and Paugam, 2023; Giner and Luque-Luque-Vílchez, 2022). Ongoing bilateral dialogue is in place between EFRAG and ISSB to ensure interoperability between the two standards and avoid double reporting. However, the coexistence of two new prominent SR standard-setters (ISSB and EFRAG), based on different underlying objectives and requirements, "makes it increasingly difficult for both decision-makers in organizations and researchers to keep track of changes in legislation and reporting standards" (Hummel and Jobst, 2024: 321). For instance, Baboukardos et al. (2023) talk about a 'multiverse' of SR requirements.
- *limited policy coherence with the other EU corporate sustainability initiatives* that have emerged out of the EU Green Deal. In particular, despite the importance of DD in the CSRD, the ESRS was developed almost in isolation from the CSDDD initiative (Mélon, 2026). It has been argued that the EU has developed "sustainability regulations in the reverse order to what logic dictates": it should have set out mandatory sustainability due diligence rules first; then, ask companies to report about those efforts; and, finally,

define what investors needed to report about the sustainability of their portfolios (Shift, 2025). In general, CSRD/ESRS could be better integrated across a wide range of EU regulatory-driven developments (e.g. critical raw materials, battery regulation, deforestation, etc.) to encourage organisational change and avoid unnecessary administrative burden.

2.1.3 The Omnibus Regulatory U-turn and Polarised Debate

A first signal that the Commission was shifting to 'business-first policy' came already in October 2023, only months after the ESRS adoption, when President von der Leyen pledged to cut company reporting requirements by 25 per cent (European Commission, 2023). Internal and external pressures on the EU Commission to halt or water down not only the application of the CSRD rules but the whole European sustainability agenda kept escalating (e.g. Brunetti et al., 2024; Wolman & Gros, 2025), particularly after the European parliamentary elections. Eventually, von der Leyen became increasingly committed to downsizing the EU Green Dean in the name of competitiveness (European Commission, 2025a). On 26th February 2025, the EU Commission completed a "dramatic U-turn on corporate green rules" (Gros, 2025) by releasing a much-anticipated and far-reaching Omnibus I and II 'simplification package', deeply affecting the CSRD as well as other corporate sustainability laws (the CSDDD and Taxonomy regulation) (European Commission, 2025b).

The main changes proposed in the Omnibus concerning corporate sustainability disclosure are:

- two-year delay for companies that have not yet reported but remain in the CSRD scope;
- The scope of the CSRD and Taxonomy is aligned with CSDDD (only companies above 1000 employees), which represents a removal of approximately 80 per cent of companies from the original scope. Instead large companies are encouraged to adopt voluntary SR;
- ESRS are reviewed for streamlining – proposes reducing by half the number of data points companies must collect, and dropping sector-specific reporting standards due in 2026;
- CSDDD requirements are also delayed by one year and due diligence is only required on direct business partners (tier 1) while the frequency of assessment is relaxed from annual to five years;
- Other aspects of the CSDDD are also watered down: penalties are softened by removing the link to percentage of net turnover; climate transition plans need

to be merely 'adopted' rather than 'put into effect'; EU-wide civil liability is removed and the decision is left to Member State-level;
- A financial materiality threshold is introduced for the Taxonomy reporting, reducing the reporting templates by 70 per cent as well as a simplification of the 'Do No Significant Harm" (DNSH) criteria related to pollution prevention and the use of chemicals.

At the time of completing the writing of this work (May 2025), it is impossible to anticipate what will be the outcome of the Omnibus legislative negotiation. If approved, the Commission's proposal could undermine the effectiveness of the new European standards for SR. As noted by the European Central Bank in its formal opinion (ECB, 2025), it would "significantly limit stakeholders' access to important information" and the proposed reduction in scope "would reduce the overall availability of sustainability-related information, including information on GHG emissions produced by undertakings". Many fear that this represents a setback not only for SR regulation but for the EU ambition to lead the transition to a sustainable and resource-efficient economic model (UNPRI, IIGCC, Eurosif, 2025; ECB, 2025).

What is particularly striking is the inconsistency of the European Commission's approach to corporate sustainability and accountability under the leadership of von der Leyen. During the Omnibus press conference, Commissioner Dombrovskis (2025) stigmatised as "very burdensome reporting" the very requirements that he and his team developed and actively promoted (e.g. increasing trust in business, creating legal certainty, improving risk management and resilience, and increasing competitiveness). Pascal Canfin, a centrist French MEP, reacted to the Omnibus by saying, "Today is a contradictory day for European climate action" (European Parliament, 2025) and Beate Beller (Global Witness) said "Commission President von der Leyen's attack on her own sustainability agenda is disgraceful" (Gros, 2025). Simon Mundy, who covers sustainability issues for the *Financial Times*, noted that "the hasty slashing of laws passed only recently, and which have not yet even been fully implemented, smacks of inconsistency" (2025).

The reactions that followed the Omnibus proposal illustrate a growing polarisation in the public debate on mandatory SR (Braun, 2025), revealing tensions and trade-offs that had been hidden under the dominant depoliticised view taken by the EU. Predictably, trade associations such as the European Round Table for Industry (ERT), FuelsEurope, BusinessEurope, and SMEunited expressed strong support for "simplification", while NGOs such as Global Witness, Friends of the Earth, and Human Rights Watch call it irresponsible and aggressive "deregulation" (ERT, 2025; ECCJ, 2025; Braun, 2025). However, it would be a mistake to frame it as the usual clash between business and civil society. Many SMEs and also major corporations, such as IKEA, Ferrero, Nestlé, Unilever, and l'Oréal, publicly took a position against the Omnibus (ERT, 2025; IDVO, 2025). Investor associations representing over €6.6 trillion assets under management issued a joint statement asking the Commission to preserve the integrity and ambition of the EU reporting framework (UNPRI, IIGCC, Eurosif, 2025). In stark contrast to the years of evidence gathering, public consultations, and balanced negotiations that shaped the targeted EU laws, many have highlighted the lack of transparency and undue haste that has characterised the fast-track decision by the Commission to adopt the Omnibus (WWF, 2025; ECCJ, 2025). An analysis of the demands made by key business associations in their letters and position papers shows significant similarities with the Commission's Omnibus proposal (ReclaimFinance, 2025). Thus, in April 2025, eight NGOs submitted a formal complaint with the European Ombudsman, condemning the undemocratic, untransparent, and rushed way in which the European Commission has developed the Omnibus proposal (FoE, 2025). As noted by MEP Lara Wolters (European Parliament, 2025), "this is not the simplification of EU rules. This is the simplification of a debate". von der Leyen's sudden deregulation turn and mixed signals risk disorienting investors and the many companies that have invested time and resources not only in compliance but preparing for the resource-efficient and climate-neutral future promised in the European Green Deal. I agree with Andreas Rasche and Georg Kell (2025) the need for moving from a cost to a value narrative, based on a new post-Omnibus sustainability narrative that does "clarify why sustainability reporting and due diligence matter".

This research takes a step back from current heated debates about the Omnibus and contextualises it as part of the historical development of SR regulation in Europe, linking it with long-term changes in corporate governance and value creation regimes. While the current U-turn might have been particularly troublesome, by all means it is not the first or the only one in the history of European SR regulation. As illustrated in the following section, the Omnibus has been only the latest instance in a series of U-turns, regulatory captures, and regulatory failures that mark the history of accounting for sustainability. Thus, the urgent question that needs to be addressed concerns the underlying structural problems that explain this recursive regulatory failure and what can be learnt from past experience.

2.2 The Argument in Brief: The Fallacy of Sustainability Reporting

In this Element, I argue that the current accounting rules, and their underlying notions of value, are not fit for purpose and they have repeatedly failed to serve long-term sustainability goals because of a structural fallacy in the design of SR regulation. Such fallacy consists in narrowly defining accounting as merely technical, monolithic, and stable representations of micro-level organisational practices, detached from large economic, societal, and ecological questions (Chapman et al., 2009). This conventional "restrictive view" (Zambon, 2002: 26) of accounting has been instrumental in designing SR regulation as external and extraneous to financial reporting. Thus, instead of transforming accounting standards, ultimately demands for SR regulation have been marginalised and isolated, framed as secondary, merely an add-on to extant accounting standards. Drawing on a longstanding tradition of sociological and political economic accounting research (Tinker, 1980; Hopwood and Miller, 1994; Hopwood, 2007; Perry and Nölke, 2006; Botzem, 2012; Miller and Power, 2013), I suggest characterising *accounting as a powerful tool for political economy having socio-ecological systemic effects that can be leveraged to achieve constitutional sustainability objectives*. Crucially, here sustainability is not a set of additional KPIs or information about sustainability to be – eventually – added to existing financial information. It is a set of overarching morally committed and political constitutional objectives (Kampourakis, 2018; Khaitan, 2019; Herlin-Karnell, 2023) that require fundamentally rethinking accounting rules and, consequently, our financialised, predatory approach to value creation (Strange, 1996; Epstein, 2005; Lazonick and Shin, 2019; Lazonick, 2023)

In contrast to a conventional depoliticised and decontextualised view of accounting standards, it is time to acknowledge the normative nature of accounting and its power in shaping larger socio-economic and ecological processes through calculations (Hopwood, 1983; Carruthers and Espeland, 2012). Historians have indeed shown that accounting has had a remarkable impact on the rise and fall of entire nations and the construction of modern capitalism. Various thinkers such as Weber, Shumpeter, and Sombart already stressed the close link between calculability, accounting, and the emergence and evolution of capitalist societies and modern (economic) rationality (see Carruthers and Espelands, 2012). According to Weber, "[t]he most general presupposition for the existence of this present-day capitalism is that of rational capital accounting as the norm for all large industrial undertakings which are concerned with provision for everyday wants" (Weber [1927] 1981: 276). Sombart even claimed that "one can say that capital, as a category, did not exist before double-entry bookkeeping. Capital can be defined as that amount of wealth which is used in making profits and which enters into the accounts" (Sombart, 1953: 38). Contemporary sociological studies of accounting emphasise "the mutually constitutive nature of accounting, organizing, and economizing" (Miller and Power, 2013: 557). They contend that "accounting is much more constructive than reflective of social values; more active than passive in social ordering" (Fleischman 2004: 18). Rather than there being an 'economic realm' which is independent of and pre-exists accounting, the relationship is reversed or, at least, much more dialectic (Hopwood, 1992; Mennicken and Power, 2015; Vollmer, 2024). For instance, Klamer and McCloskey note that economics "is dominated by accounting ideas. . . . in fact their field is ruled by little else" (1992: 145–146).

Thus, the field of accounting shapes and is shaped by wider changes in corporate governance regimes and capital accumulation (Jessop 1992 and 2007; Aglietta and Reberioux, 2005; Fligstein and Shin, 2004; Streeck, 2011; Lazonick & Shin, 2019). As discussed in Section 3, changes in accounting standards – in particular the wide adoption of IFRS – have played a crucial role in the parallel process of financialisation of the economy which became particularly acute in the 1990s and 2000s (Perry and Nölke, 2006; Djelic & Sahlin, 2009; Chiapello, 2015, 2016). The latter has been instrumental in establishing and strengthening an economic order, characterised by what Lazonick defines as a 'predatory' model of value creation (Lazonick and Shin, 2019; Lazonick, 2023). Ultimately, I argue that the emergence of global, privatised financial market-driven accounting standards co-evolved with the progressive financialisation of the economy (Botzem, 2012; Ramanna, 2015). In this perspective, demands for mandatory SR regulation can be explained as a reaction to the hyper-financialisation and privatisation of accounting rules and a (so far largely unsuccessful) attempt to correct this trend.

There is evidence that the adoption of IFRS accounting rules is linked to increased risks of socio-economic and ecological unsustainability (e.g. Palea, 2018 and 2022; Haldane et al., 2024). IFRS have led to a disconnection between wages and productivity (Palea, 2018; Shipman, 2015; Sikka, 2015), which in its turn has promoted household debt to sustain consumption levels, thus leading to a decline of the working class (Hein et al., 2016). Recent research (Haldane et al., 2024) demonstrates that underinvestment under IFRS has proved to negatively impact climate change mitigation pathways (Haldane et al., 2024). A new awareness of the socio-ecological crisis – driven by sustainability science and societal demands for accountability – is delegitimising and weakening conventional accounting practices, forcing regulators to take into consideration both social and environmental externalities. Ultimately, this promises to have consequences on the whole economic order. As opposed to the silo distinction between financial and sustainability accounting, there is a need for a more comprehensive, normative notion of accounting contributing towards a regenerative economy (Lyle, 1996; Raworth, 2017; Brand-Correa et al., 2022; Kallis et al., 2025). This entails bridging critical accounting studies, political economic studies of predatory financialised capitalism, and the literature on the roots and effects of the current socio-ecological crisis.

Far from being only a legitimising tool for corporate power (Cho et al., 2012), effective SR regulation can be potentially creative of a new regime of "economic governance – not just corporate governance, though it has implications for that, but also governance of the economy and even of society at large" (Mclean and Crouch, 2012: 1). This perspective points to the importance of studying historically specific 'constellations' (Burchell et al., 1980), meaning the particular social field where a set of diverse practices, processes, and institutions intersected and evolved. I share Hopwood's view that "[a]ccounting has been a craft that has had no essence. It has changed significantly across time, adopting new forms, methods, and roles" (Hopwood, 2007: 1367). Here accounting is seen both as a 'performative' communicative and calculative practice that defines and creates social relations and as a set of open, plastic, and reconfigurable tools that do not have a purpose, but can be made purposeful (Miller and Rose, 1990; Hopwood and Miller, 1994; Mennicken and Power, 2015). Following this approach, I understand the long-term development of SR regulation – its variety of rationales and definitions (see Section 2.2) – as part of recursive struggles for changing the institutionalised field of accounting to include social and environmental matters. Peter Miller (1998) argues that it is

> at the margins that accounting as a body of legitimated practices is formed and re-formed by the adding of devices and ideas of various kinds. It is at the margins that accounting intersects with, and comes into conflict with, other bodies of expertise. And it is at the margins that accounting comes to be linked up to the demands, expectations and ideals of diverse social and institutional agencies. (Miller, 1998: 174)

Accordingly, I see the marginalisation of SR practices and struggles for its inclusion in accounting standards and regulation as part of the ongoing problematisation of accounting practices and thus a manifestation of concern with the conditions and consequences of mainstream accounting practices.

This argument puts to the fore the analysis of the ways in which SR practices "have been formed historically, what conditions made them possible, what ideals and aspirations they embody, and how they seek to programme the world so as to fit these ideals" (Miller, 1998: 177). The following section will expand on this standpoint by providing a long-term overview of changes in SR regulation over an extended period of time (from the 1960s to date).

2.3 Methodological Considerations

Defining SR practices is notoriously challenging, because SR can take different forms and can be directed at diverse audiences. The content of such reports might concern matters as diverse as carbon emission, labour rights, biodiversity, water usage, health and safety, human rights, diversity and inclusion, and bribery and corruption. Furthermore, it also cuts across issues related to accounting for intangible assets, such as reputation and brand value, and human capital and training. Aspects of corporate performance covered in SR are often specific to each particular company and to the context in which they operate. Therefore, reporting varies from company to company, resulting in inconsistencies across them (Cooper and Michelon, 2022; Archer, 2024; Hardyment, 2024). Thus, Gray (2010: 546) could argue that to try and talk about SR "as a singularity is to invite confusion". This plurality of views about SR is reflected in the many ways in which this business practice has been defined over time: social accounting, CSR reports, non-financial reporting, sustainability reporting and ESG information. This lack of a unified and clear definition is what I call the 'SR conundrum' and it constitutes a major challenge for regulating SR.

Instead of simply choosing one of the existing definitions of SR or even creating a new one, I take a reflexive historical approach, analysing SR as a social practice in search of a definition and regulation as a major force for harmonising different practices and approaches.

Drawing on Bourdieu, a reflexive approach "signifies a scientific process of uncovering the agents' orientations, and the predispositions shaping their habits and practices" (Madsen and Dezalay 2002: 190; see Bourdieu 1984; 1996). Without going into the details of this approach, the key aim of this 'reflexive' strategy is to construct a scientifically more autonomous object of research which is not based on intuitive readings or readily available classifications. In particular this study deploys what Bourdieu called the 'double historicisation' method, as a way to 'objectivise the research object' (Bourdieu, 1984, 1996). As mentioned in the Introduction, this is a research strategy aimed at revealing how both the research object – the regulation of SR in Europe – and the collective constructions of the meaning of this object have come about. The aim is not limited to relativise such tradition, putting it into a historical context; it also implies "giving back their necessity by tearing them out of the indeterminacy which stems from a false externalisation and relating them back to the social conditions of their genesis" (Bourdieu, 1996: 298). In the context of this study, this reflexive methodology helped me to uncover the relationship between financial accounting and sustainability, overcoming a number of widely adopted pre-defined *distinctions* between for example, 'financial' and 'non-financial reporting'; 'accountancy' and 'law'; 'societal', 'economic', and 'ecological' matters. A Bourdieusian reflexive 'polycentric approach' contains untapped intellectual resources to explore undergoing regulatory transformations not excluding any of the co-producers of these changes, helping to explain the recursive evolution of SR regulation. It contributes, above all, to overcome the main challenge that characterises the current public and academic debate on the regulation of SR, namely, the *definition of the object of study*.

Empirically, this work is based on over ten years of research on the EU regulation of SR (Monciardini, 2013; Monciardini, 2016; Monciardini and Conaldi, 2019; Biondi et al., 2020; Monciardini et al., 2020; Maher et al., 2020; Ahlström and Monciardini, 2022; Monciardini and Mähönen, 2026), which have informed this contribution in a considerably updated and necessarily concise form. The aim of this methodological perspective (Bourdieu, 1996; Dezalay and Madsen, 2012) is to break up the 'official stories' about the development of SR regulation into overlapping and, often, opposing texts, versions, and sources. A 'double historicisation' allows to put together the various pieces of the SR conundrum by showing that "these conflicting narratives ultimately reflect its many stakes, as well as they highlight the central conflicts of its historical progression" (Madsen, 2006: 38). As different groups of actors and social constituencies have conflicting normative ideas about which information is relevant to the measurement and disclosure of corporate performance, it is the collective process of shaping the very meaning of this social practice that becomes a central element of study (see Sections 3 and 4). The key contribution of this study is to juxtapose and critically assess the main responses to the questions: What does regulating SR mean?

3 History of Sustainability Reporting

It has become commonplace to argue that there has been a linear and progressive development from corporate 'irresponsibility' towards an epoch of greater corporate accountability and sustainability. Thus, mandatory SR has been often framed as "an idea whose time has come" (Spofforth, 2012: 18), signalling the inevitable coming of age of 'stakeholder' or 'sustainable' capitalism (Fink, 2018; Business Roundtable, 2019). However, there are various issues with this deterministic explanation of SR emergence. First of all, it neglects the role of interests and conflicts in shaping the corporate field. Furthermore, as briefly outlined throughout this section, a more careful historical analysis reveals that the debate on mandatory SR was more developed and lively in the 1970s than in the 1990s and it finally re-emerged only in the late 2000s. This conclusion suggests a cyclical rather than linear and progressive development of SR regulation. In particular, the brief historical account offered by this section draws attention to the necessity of rethinking the development of SR regulation within the history of accounting regulation and of broader changes in the political-economic and ecological context.

The practice of corporate SR has a long history. However, as noted by prior analyses (Mathews, 1997; Owen, 2008; Buhr et al., 2014; Magnan and Michelon, 2024), most of the literature lacks historical depth. Broadly speaking, in the European context, we can identify three major waves through which the current regulatory landscape has been shaped. After an initial SR regulation wave in the 1960s–1970s in which SR legislations were widely discussed as part of national industrial relations, by the 1980s this debate suddenly came to an end without producing significant legislative changes. Regulatory debates re-emerged in the 1990s–2000s but, again, regulators failed to deliver on initial intentions to enhance comparability, consistency, and integration of information. Sustainability issues – significantly called 'non-financials' – were marginalised or entirely excluded from regulatory debates about amending EU accounting rules or updating the IFRS. Instead, between the 1990s and 2010s, dozens of competing and complementing SR voluntary standards and guidelines emerged. Therefore, despite some noticeable exceptions, such as France (Gond and Igalens, 2012), until the 2010s, in most EU jurisdictions SR was seen as a business practice that companies could freely undertake – as stated by the Commission – "over and above legal requirements" (European Commission 2002). After the 2008 financial crisis, the situation has gradually changed. Particularly in Europe but also globally, we are witnessing a shift towards mandatory reporting and harmonisation of SR standards, seen as a risk management tool in the current socio-ecological crisis.

This section questions what explains this cyclical and recursive development. The aim is to learn from the past, because – after over fifty years of fruitless debates – we cannot afford another regulatory failure and capture of the SR agenda (Biondi et al., 2020).

3.1 1960s–1980s: The Rise and Fall of Social Accounting

Firstly, the original wave of 'social reporting' emerged in the 1960s and 1970s, led by governmental initiatives and mainly concerned with social and labour-related information, neglecting the environmental side. This debate is closely related to the political-economic and corporate governance regime that characterised the post-war period of economic Keynesianism and European corporatist industrial relations. During this phase, the economy was largely under political control. In Europe, the very concept of 'corporate governance' was seen as a sub-system of the state's 'governance of the economy', organised through a triangular partnership of coordinated industrial relations between employers and employees, with governments playing a key role as the 'social bargain' facilitators.

It is in this broader socio-economic context that first emerged in Europe a lively debate about the need for creating a set of standards and practices for mandatory corporate social accounting. According to Dierkes (1979), in the Federal Republic of West Germany, 50 per cent of the largest companies were reporting on their social performance, although only in forty to sixty cases this practice is defined as methodologically 'at a quite advanced level'. According to Rey (1980), in France the percentage of large companies disclosing social information was even higher (see also Chevalier 1976). He maintained that an estimated 200 to 300 companies were already involved in social reporting before 1977, when this practice became mandatory for all French firms above 300 employees. At the time, social accounting was seen by trade unions as a means "to increase the control of labour unions on business affairs" (Ullmann, 1979: 130). On the other hand, corporate owners and management saw social reporting as a means to deal with the growing influence of organised labour and to legitimise their position during a period of intensified social conflicts.

Focusing on regulatory aspects, proposals for social accounting legislation were widely debated across different European jurisdictions, particularly in France, the UK, and West Germany; however, in most of the cases, they failed to produce actual legislative changes. The example par excellence of the social accounting regulation that characterised this period is the introduction in 1977 in France of the *bilan social* by the 77-769 Law (see Gond and Igalens, 2012). Strongly supported by President Valéry Giscard d'Estaing, this legislation mandates large companies to prepare a social account annually and submit it to a committee of workers and managers that have to discuss and approve it. The law was highly prescriptive and mandated companies to prepare a report based on 134 quantitative and statistical measures and indicators, including chapters on employment, training, health and safety, labour relations, working conditions, and living conditions (see Harribey, 2009). In the UK, the Accounting Standards Steering Committee published, in 1975, the far-reaching *The Corporate Report*, which aimed to "re-examine the scope and aims of published financial reports in the lights of modern needs and condition" (ASSC, 1975). This cutting-edge discussion paper constitutes an extraordinary document of the kind of debate that characterised this period, not only in Continental Europe but also in the UK, particularly because its focus was not on corporate social accounting but on accounting practices in general. It states, for instance, that "recognition of changes in public attitude" is leading to a "trend in recent proposed and actual legislation towards the imposition of disclosure requirements not directly linked to the needs of shareholders", which are "likely to lead to a greater recognition in company law of the rights of employees" (pp. 39–40). The Report clearly states that profit maximisation for shareholders represents the past: "Because neither business nor the public regards the maximisation of owners' profit as the only legitimate aim of business, distributable profits can no longer be regarded as the sole or premier indicator of performance" (p. 38). The Report includes a detailed explanation of prospective changes in accounting requirements and identifies several issues that need further research. It concludes: "We recognise the trend in new and proposed legislations towards the recognition of the rights to information of a growing number of groups including employees and the public. We recognise there is need for additional indicators of performance in the corporate reports of all entities" (p. 75). At the international level, this first wave also produced the Organisation for Economic Co-operation and Development (OECD) Guidelines for Multinational Enterprises. While the Guidelines were subsequently revised and expanded over time, it is interesting to highlight that the focus of the original declaration on employment and industrial relations reflects the spirit of the time and the power of trade unions, with a notable absence of environmental issues (see Hägg, 1984).

At the beginning of the 1980s, this international regulatory debate suddenly came to an end. As a consequence, SR came to be widely conceived only as a market-led practice, adopted by corporations on a purely voluntary and discretionary basis (Unerman et al., 2007; Gray et al., 2009).

3.2 1990s–2010s: Corporate Social Accountability and CSR Reporting

A second wave of SR regulatory initiatives emerged in the late 1990s/early 2000s, resulting in the adoption of a number of voluntary frameworks, including in particular the Eco-Management and Audit Scheme (EMAS) (1993), the influential Global Reporting Initiative (GRI) (1996), the UN Global Compact (UNGP) (2000), and the Carbon Disclosure Project (CDP) (2000).

By the turn of the millennium, European public authorities were adamant about the need for changing accounting rules to introduce mandatory SR (European Union, 1978, 1983). This is evident in the 2001 Recommendation of the EU Commission on the recognition, measurement, and disclosure of environmental issues in the annual accounts and reports of companies. It states, The lack of explicit rules has contributed to a situation where different stakeholders, including regulatory authorities, investors, financial analysts and the public in general may consider the environmental information disclosed by companies to be either inadequate or unreliable ... In the absence of harmonised authoritative guidelines in relation to environmental issues and financial reporting, comparability between companies becomes difficult. ... The information is often disclosed in a variety of non-harmonised ways among companies and/or reporting periods, rather than being presented in an integrated and consistent manner throughout the annual accounts and the annual report. (European Commission, 2001). Since accounting legislation had become, in the meantime, competence of European regulators, the Commission was tasked to follow up on the 2001 Recommendation as part of a wider strategy for strengthening corporate social accountability and responsibility.

Breaking with the tripartite social dialogue between public authorities, employers, and unions that had characterised European industrial relations until the mid-1990s, the Commission adopted a multi-stakeholder regulatory approach (Fairbrass, 2011; Monciardini and Conaldi, 2019). Thus, an EU Multi-Stakeholder Forum on Corporate Social Responsibility (CSR) (2002–2004) was established to foster dialogue and voluntary CSR initiatives, particularly in the area of transparency and accountability. As already analysed in the literature, this regulatory process failed to deliver any major progress and eventually was manifestly captured by the regulatory target, large companies (de Schutter, 2008; Ungericht and Hirt, 2010; Fairbrass, 2011; Kinderman, 2013, 2016; Monciardini and Conaldi, 2019). While companies could decide to include social and environmental information in some sections of their mandatory annual reports, they were not required by law to do so (e.g. UK Management Discussion and Analysis; EU Modernisation Directive). Business organisations could decide to entirely avoid any form of SR or, alternatively, to cherry-pick and even fabricate positive information to be included in glossy reports aimed at strengthening their social and environmental credentials (Solomon et al., 2013; Diouf and Boiral, 2017).

As a consequence of this hands-off approach by EU policy-makers, the SR landscape has been characterised by an ever-expanding maze of weak and voluntary options (see Monciardini et al., 2020). While some of the voluntary SR frameworks that emerge during this phase share similar underlying assumptions, overlaps are only partial and major differences exist across the various frameworks in relation to crucial issues such as the legitimacy of the standard-setting bodies, the definition of materiality, the users towards which the reporting framework is oriented, the thematic aspects included, and the key principles or more detailed set of KPIs adopted. At the same time, all frameworks have certain aspects in common that reflect the historical neoliberal economic context (Moon, 2004; Harvey, 2007; Albareda et al., 2008; Kinderman, 2012):

- In line with a period marked by the neoliberal 'retreat of the state' (Strange, 1996), voluntary standards were filling the void due to the lack of legislative SR initiatives;

- Because of the above, the only means available to prompt companies to voluntarily disclose was to demonstrate that there is a link between SR and a competitive advantage, for example, reputational rewards. Thus, underpinning this SR frame-working exercise is the so-called 'business case' for CSR ('doing well by doing good') and an instrumental approach to corporate responsibility;
- Compared to the first wave of the 1970s, there is a stronger emphasis on environmental issues, as illustrated in particular by EMAS and CDP, which focus exclusively on these. The original focus on employees and trade unions information needs is then extended to other stakeholders, in particular CSOs. However, the former focus on employees and social dialogue was lost.

3.3 2010s–Date: Socio-ecological Crisis and SR Standardisation

A third wave (or layer) of SR regulation originated after the 2008 global financial crisis, breaking with the laissez-faire and voluntary approaches to business regulation that characterised the previous period (Knudsen and Moon, 2017 and 2022; Monciardini and Conaldi, 2019; Kourula et al., 2019). However, the real driver of this regulatory shift has been the overwhelming scientific evidence on the severity of the current socio-ecological crisis and its link with corporate (mis)behaviour (e.g. Adams and Abhayawansa, 2022; Callahan and Mankin, 2025). This shift comes together with unprecedented recognition that sustainability-related information is becoming increasingly material for all sorts of investors, not only "responsible investors" (e.g. Friede et al., 2015; Eccles and Klimenko 2019; Ahlström and Monciardini, 2022).

At national level, legislative initiatives aimed at enhancing corporate public accountability have been adopted, such as the 2010 Grenelle II Law and the 'Devoir de Vigilance' Law in France, and the 2013 Companies Act and 2015 Modern Slavery Act in the UK (see Knudsen et al., 2015; Kourula et al., 2019; La Torre et al., 2018; Monciardini and Conaldi, 2019). At the European level, in 2014, the European Union introduced a requirement for mandatory SR – the EU Non Financial Reporting Directive (hereon NFRD) (European Union, 2014) – amending the consolidated Accounting Directive (European Union, 2013). In the NFRD Impact Assessment, European public authorities (European Commission, 2013) explained that "the pace of progress towards more transparent disclosure practices remains slow, and a majority of users (including in particular investors, NGOs and other civil society organisations) consider the current level of transparency in this field as unable to meet their needs. Specific issues have been highlighted with regard to both quantity and quality of information available". As already explained in Section 2, the NFRD was further amended in 2023 with the adoption of the more stringent CSRD, mandating large companies active in the EU to issue SR according to a new set of European Sustainability Reporting Standards (ESRS). This new regulatory momentum has been followed through, at the international level, by a variety of new relevant frameworks and the profound revision of some of the existing ones (such as the OECD Guidelines and the GRI). New SR initiatives include, in particular:

- ISO 26000 Social Responsibility Standard issued in 2010 by the International Organisation for Standardisation (ISO), the world's largest developer and publisher of standards;
- UN Guiding Principles on Business and Human Rights (UNGP, also known as the 'Protect, Respect and Remedy' Framework) that have been endorsed by the UN Human Rights Council (UN HRC) in 2011;
- International Integrated Reporting Framework (IRF) issued by the International Integrated Reporting Council (IIRC) in 2014;
- The seventeen Sustainable Development Goals (SDGs) set in 2015 by the United Nations General Assembly and intended to be a "blueprint to achieve a better and more sustainable future for all";
- The Science Based Targets initiative (SBTi), established in 2015 to help companies to set emission reduction targets in line with climate science and Paris Agreement goals;
- Recommendations issued in 2017 by the Task Force on Climate-related Financial Disclosures (TCFD), developed by the Financial Stability Board;
- The Sustainable Development Performance Indicators (SDPIs), first released in November 2022 by the United Nations Research Institute for Social Development (UNRISD);
- IFRS Sustainability Disclosure Standards (IFRS S), first released in 2023.

Arguably, the most significant initiatives that are characterising this phase have been the EU's introduction of mandatory SR, followed by the creation of the IFRS S (Cooper and Michelon, 2022; Hummel and Jobst, 2024; Bohn et al., 2025).

In 2009 the EU Commission started a torn regulatory process that, only in 2014, resulted in the adoption of the NFRD (European Union, 2014; Kinderman, 2019). The stance of the EU was that SR is "vital to managing change towards a sustainable global economy by combining long-term profitability with social justice and environmental protection" (European Union, 2014). For the first time, over 11,000 corporations in the European Economic Area were mandated to publish a SR on their policies, risks, and outcomes regarding environmental, social, and human rights matters. The NFRD takes a multi-stakeholder approach to SR, meeting the information needs of different stakeholders, not only financial capital providers. While its adoption constitutes an important step forward (Monciardini and Conaldi, 2019), there is evidence that the initial ambition of the Commission to tackle sustainability issues was significantly "weakened during the course of the negotiations" (Kinderman, 2019: 675). As acknowledged by Commissioner Barnier, the EU "made substantial efforts to ensure that the administrative burden imposed on companies is minimal" (Barnier, 2014: 18). In many ways, it is hard to imagine more favourable circumstances for SR regulation, due to the mix of financial and ecological crises (Kinderman, 2019). As shown by Monciardini and Conaldi (2019), the NFRS was supported by a wide and unprecedented 'coalition of the unlikely', including not only the 'usual suspects' – trade unions and civil society – but also a surprising share of institutional and responsible investors. This alignment of all the main users of SR information, demanding for more stringent accountability rules, has been crucial to break the narrative that mandatory SR is an 'anti-business' measure (Monciardini 2016; Monciardini and Conaldi, 2019). Nonetheless, according to one of its negotiators, Stefanos Komninos, the proposal was "close to failing" and it was "very difficult to negotiate this Directive" (in Kinderman, 2019: 675). Ultimately, by maintaining a very broad and generic approach, the NFRD did fail to achieve its intended objective "to increase the relevance, consistency and comparability" of information disclosed by large corporations across the European Union. Limitations in terms of quality and quantity of information disclosed were soon exposed by large-scale assessments of corporate compliance with the NFRD (Alliance for Corporate Transparency, 2020; ESMA, 2020).

As already discussed in Section 2, following the adoption of the EU Commission Sustainable Finance Action Plan (European Commission, 2018) and, in particular, the European Green Deal (European Commission, 2019), there was a renewed, wide and shared consensus that the shortcomings of the NFRD needed to be addressed. This led to the adoption, in December 2022, of the CSRD (European Union, 2022). The CSRD underlines that "In the absence of policy action, the gap between users' information needs and the sustainability information provided by undertakings is expected to grow. That gap has significant negative consequences" (European Union, 2022: para 14). Thus, the CSRD significantly expands the scope of the NFRD to about 50,000 corporate organisations, maintaining a stakeholder-based approach, and expanding the NFRD requirements. The first set of ESRS was published by EFRAG in December 2023 (European Commission, 2023). The adoption of the CSRD/ESRS constitutes an historical step change, opening up a public debate on how the standards on SR should be undertaken henceforth. However, once again, there has been formidable opposition and lobbying for weakening the adoption of the CSRD regulation and delaying or halting its implementation. Finally, in 2025, the European Commission issued the Omnibus proposal which risks substantially reducing the quality and quantity of SR information that companies are required to publish under the ESRS. As warned by the vice-chair of the supervisory board of the European Central Bank (ECB), Frank Elderson, "The debate on competitiveness should not be used as a pretext for watering down regulation" (Arnold, 2025). EFRAG was given only few months (April–October 2025) to: (a) "substantially reduce the number of ESRS datapoints", (b) provide "clearer instruction on how to apply the materiality principle", and (c) "improve consistency with other pieces of EU legislation" and ensure a "high degree of interoperability with other global sustainability reporting standards" (European Commission, 2025). It is important to note that the revision of the ESRS is taking place under immense stress, due to time pressure and the uncertainty around the outcome of the negotiations between EU co-legislators. The Commission expects that firms which report for financial year 2027 can use the revised standards.

Simultaneously, the IFRS Foundation, under which the International Accounting Standards Board (IASB) issues the IFRS, turned its attention to sustainability standards. The creation of the ISSB was announced in November 2021 at the United Nations Climate Change Conference (COP26). The IFRS Foundation formalised the appointment of Emmanuel Faber (CEO of Danone) as ISSB chair in December 2021. In late March 2022, the ISSB published its first two exposure drafts, respectively on climate and general sustainability-related financial disclosures. The first two Sustainability Disclosure Standards, IFRS S1 General Requirements for Disclosure of Sustainability-related Financial Information and IFRS S2 Climate-related Disclosures, were published in June 2023. So far, the main impact of the creation of the ISSB has been a convergence of the multitude of voluntary SR standards. Namely, four prominent sustainability reporting organisations (TCFD, CDSB, IIRC and SASB) have consolidated into the work of the ISSB. The ISSB has faced substantial criticism, particularly for its prioritisation of investor interest over other stakeholders (Adams and Mueller, 2022; Ali et al., 2023; de Villiers et al., 2024; Bohn et al., 2025). However, as noted by de Villiers and colleagues (2024: 269), "the current and potential influence of the ISSB as a global reporting body is substantial". The aim is clearly to repeat what happened in the early 2000s with corporate financial reporting and to obtain that the EU Commission and other policymakers adopt the IFRS S as the basis for mandatory SR in their jurisdictions.

Since this third wave of SR standards is still ongoing at the moment of writing this work, it is too early to fully grasp its implications. However, one can already identify certain underlying patterns that mark a breakthrough as compared to the prior two waves:

- As compared to the plethora of voluntary standards that emerged between 1990s and until the 2008 financial crisis, this new phase is characterised by legislative-driven SR initiatives. The public debate has shifted from *whether* to *how* SR should be regulated. This is resulting in an ongoing process of harmonisation of SR;
- Following on the prior point, we are witnessing a 'war of standards' between public as well as private standard-setters and across different views of SR for the definition of key issues such as: the legitimacy of the standard-setting bodies, the definition of materiality, the users towards which the reporting framework is oriented, the thematic aspects included, and the key principles or more detailed set of KPIs adopted.
- The most significant fault line is between the ISSB (issuing IFRS sustainability standards), which advocates SR limited to financially material sustainability information designed for financial capital providers ("single materiality"), and the CSRD approach, which supports a multi-stakeholder approach and a broader idea of materiality ("double materiality"). The latter aims to include both information about how a corporate entity is impacted by sustainability issues ("outside-in") and how their activities impact society and the environment ("inside-out") (Cooper and Michelon, 2022; Mähönen and Palea, 2024).
- It is crucial to highlight that new private standard-setters such as the IIRC and lately the ISSB – which aims to develop globally accepted frameworks for SR – lack legitimacy and authority, and, without a legal endorsement, are adopted by a relatively small number of companies. At the same time, legally binding obligations for SR, which have the aim of addressing the failures of these types of voluntary regulation, run the risk of creating further fragmentation and higher administrative costs for corporations operating across different jurisdictions. The result so far has been the emergence of a mixed regime for reporting that combines voluntary and mandatory elements.
- If the previous two waves were driven respectively by the information needs of organised labour and civil society, it is increasingly clear that during the current phase, so-called 'responsible investors' and their demands for reliable ESG information have come to play a key role. After decades characterised by the financialisation of the global economy (Epstein, 2005; Strange, 2015), this is hardly surprising and again reflects the spirit of our times. The financial sector has accumulated immense leverage and influence on corporations, political leaders, and organised civil society (Cerrato and Ferrando, 2020). At the same time, following the 2008 financial crisis, finance had been in the

eye of the storm and under growing public scrutiny and regulatory pressure. Thus, investor-driven SR initiatives aimed at enhancing transparency and tackling climate issues and human rights violations (e.g. TCFD; IIRC; SBTi; ISSB) represented also a way to regain (and maintain) social legitimacy (Ahlström and Monciardini, 2021). For instance, investors had a prominent role in the 2015 Paris Agreement.

4 Putting the Pieces Together: What Explains Changes?

What explains the cyclical development of SR regulatory waves, its sudden disappearance from the political agenda in the 1980s, and equally rapid re-emergence in the 2000s and then in the 2010s? What explains the extended struggles, recursive regulatory capture, and weak regulatory outcomes that characterise this history?

While the SR regulatory debate has been traditionally analysed in isolation from contemporary developments in financial reporting regulation, I suggest that these areas could be better understood if considered together, in the context of broader changes in the socio-economic context. In line with the underlying theoretical perspective outlined in Section 2.2, emphasising "the mutually constitutive nature of accounting, organizing, and economizing" (Miller and Power, 2013: 557), there is a co-evolution of changes in accounting and in the broader organisation of the economy (Klamer and McCloskey, 1992; Biondi and Zambon, 2013). The underlying assumption is that the analysis of changes in SR regulation should be anchored in the study of corporate governance, seen as the 'architecture of accountability' of large corporations (Parkinson, 2006; Jessop, 1992 and 2007; Gourevitch and Shinn, 2005; Horn, 2011; Clarke, 2024). As noted by Newell (2008), reporting rules are particularly relevant for a responsible corporate governance because they implicitly outline the division of rights and responsibilities among civil society, states, and market actors and some of the means for achieving them. It is beyond the scope and space of this work to provide a detailed analysis of this complex co-evolution. Here, I will concentrate only on the most important turning points needed to understand major changes in SR regulation.

4.1 The End of Social Accounting and Harmonisation of Financial Accounting

First, the rise of social accounting in the 1960s–1970s and its demise starting from the 1980s can be respectively explained by looking at two elements: the dominance of a corporatist regime of corporate governance, and the harmonisation of European accounting standards.

Post-war European corporate governance and industrial relations were dominated by a 'corporatist coalition' between labour and capital (Gourevitch and Shinn, 2005. This 'historical compromise', often known as 'democratic capitalism' (Streek, 2011; Crouch, 2009 and 2011), tended to favour the alignment of interests among managers, workers, and inside owners, at the expenses of minority shareholders, sheltering companies from hostile takeovers and instability (Gourevitch and Shinn, 2005; Pagano and Volpin 2005). Corporate owners – some out of choice, others out of necessity – had to accommodate the bargaining influence of organised labour in pursuit of social peace and full employment. In many European countries, policies and laws were introduced to protect labour rights and institutionalise collective agreements. Crucially, this grand 'social bargain' functioned extraordinarily well for decades, based on the Fordist principle that higher employees' wages would benefit also the employers, because workers would be able to buy and consume more, making owners richer. It is in this context that ideas of social accounting emerged as one of the features of new models of corporate accountability based on the ideas of 'industrial democracy'. As mentioned, this possibility was considered also in the UK, often presented as a way to 'modernise' Anglo-Saxon Company Law in a period of economic downturn. The 1970s was also marking the very beginning of a public debate about limited natural resources and the "limits to growth" (e.g. Meadows et al., 1972). The introduction of social and particularly employees-related aspects was seen as a 'transformative' device which would have valued other forms of capital and empower trade unions. It was also a form of accounting that explicitly recognised the diminished role of shareholders, reduced to passive bondholders and rentiers (Ireland and Pillay, 2010).

The election of Reagan in the US and Thatcher in the UK and the rise of neoliberalism (Harvey, 2007; Kinderman, 2012; Marens, 2012) can explain why, by the end of the 1970s, this debate rapidly came to an end in Anglo-Saxon countries. However, it does not explain why the momentum for social accounting was lost also in Central European jurisdictions. I maintain that the latter can be explained by looking more closely at parallel developments in the harmonisation and internationalisation of European accounting rules (Thorell and Whittington, 1994; Hopwood, 1994; Botzem and Quack, 2005; Chiapello and Medjad, 2009). In fact, during this period, the regulatory debate increasingly moved away from national legislation – where most social accounting debates were taking place – to the EU and international level.

Until the 1980s, national accounting standards differed considerably between European countries, mirroring different economic realities (Biondi and Zambon, 2013). Broadly speaking, one major cleavage was that running between countries following the Anglo-Saxon philosophy of accounting and

Continental Europe (Nobes and Parker, 2008; Botzem and Quack, 2005; Biondi and Zambon, 2013). The two were epitomised by the UK and Germany's traditions. Broadly speaking, Anglo-Saxon accounting aimed predominantly at addressing the information needs of financial capital providers, and as a result, the emphasis was on relevance and reliability of information ('true and fair view'). They tended to be less systematically developed into statutory law. In contrast, in most Continental Europe financial accounting was closely linked with tax accounting and, as such, a powerful tool for macro political economy and public policy-making (Glaum 2000; Nobes and Parker 2008). In some countries, like Germany, annual accounting reports were the base for determining company taxation, giving priority to the prudence principle. Accounting rules were often part of the code law system (e.g. the German commercial law code) and could be changed only through legislation. In the 1970s–1980s, the European Community project of harmonising financial accounts, primarily driven by a German leadership, was complicated by the accession of the UK, Denmark, and Ireland in 1973, creating long and cumbersome negotiations (Botzem and Quack 2005). As recalled by Hopwood (1994: 243), the British accountancy profession "were worried by the potential consequences of what they saw as the imposition of continental European statutory and state control on the much more discretionary relationship between corporate management and auditor in the UK". As a result of this opposition, in 1973 they launched the International Accounting Standards Committee (IASC) – which later became the IASB. This was an international private standard-setter aimed not only at influencing the European harmonisation process towards the Anglo-Saxon approach but at establishing a globally recognised standard for financial accounting (Botzem, 2012).

For the scope of this study, what matters is that the foundation of the IASC "marked a significant shift in the development of the nascent international regulatory field of accounting" (Botzem and Quack, 2005: 8) in directions incompatible with SR regulation. In particular, it focused from the onset on developing micro-level financial accounting standards, thus, "standing in contrast to earlier macro level approaches" (Botzem and Quack, 2005: 8) characteristic of the Continental European tradition but also of 1970s social accounting regulation and OECD Guidelines for Multinational Enterprises. Furthermore, the agenda of both European regulators and the IASC was focused on the, already complicated, task of harmonising different *financial* accounting requirements. In this context, the 1970s national regulatory debates on social accounting were rapidly excluded from the legislative debate, increasingly driven by financial accounting professionals and focused on supporting the international expansion of enterprises and financial markets.

4.2 Privatised and Financialised EU Accounting Rules and CSR Reporting

By the end of the 1990s, many Continental European countries progressively abandoned the corporatist model of corporate governance, converging towards a "money concept of corporate control" (Jessop 2007; Horn, 2011; Lazonick, 2023). During this new phase, European governments decided to give up their political responsibility to guarantee full employment and made the labour market more flexible and employers free to abandon the 'collective bargain' with trade unions, in exchange for 'corporate social responsibility' (CSR) (Moon, 2004; Albareda et al., 2008) and 'privatised Keynesianism' (Crouch, 2009). Crouch defines the latter as dismantling of public welfare, compensated by unprecedented access to credit by individuals and consumers, so as to sustain full employment and more consumption (Streeck, 2011; Crouch, 2011). Hyper-financialisation and an economy based on debt allowed for more economic growth, keeping alive the promises of full employment and infinite growth implicit in post-war democratic capitalism (Streeck, 2011 and 2014).

The harmonisation and internationalisation of financial accounting rules played a key role in the financialisation of the global economy. As noted by Botzem and Quack (2005: 12), "[o]rganizational changes in the IASC have to be seen in the light of changing economic and business conditions", in particular, the increase in foreign direct investments, cross-border merger activity, and the phenomenal growth of international equity markets. The harmonisation and mutual recognition of financial reporting standards became increasingly crucial for Continental European companies aiming at gaining access to the volume and liquidity of Anglo-Saxon capital markets. Difficult negotiations took place in the 1990s across European Member States and with US accounting standard-setters (Hopwood, 1994). In the 1990s, the IASC went through a "complete overhaul of the organisational set-up" leading to its transformation into the IASB. According to Botzem and Quack (2005: 11), the aim of this transformation "was to create closer ties to national standard setters", particularly in the EU and US. The new organisation is since run by the IFRS Foundation – a not-for-profit corporation based in London and incorporated in the State of Delaware (USA) – strengthening its ties with Anglo-Saxon financial market standard setters, particularly with the International Organisation of Securities Commissions (IOSCO). Over time, Continental European professionals "diverging from the Anglo-Saxon model came increasingly under pressure to give up their accounting principles in order to raise the acceptance of IAS among financial market actors" (Botzem and Quack, 2015: 13).

Through its participation in IASC/IASB bodies, the European Commission started to consider IFRS regulation as a viable alternative to support cross-border business and financing activities. In 1995, the Commission came to the conclusion that the existing EU accounting rules did not meet the demands of preparers and users of accounts as well as those of important standard setters, particularly the FASB in the US. After long and complex debates, the EU Commission, and in particular Commissioner Bolkestein, obtained that, starting from 2005, all European listed companies were required to prepare consolidated financial reports following the shareholder-centric IFRS principles (European Union, 2002; Botzem, 2012). Together with the revision of the European Accounting Directives in line with IAS, as already mentioned in Section 2, the EU regulation created the European Financial Reporting Advisory Group (EFRAG). The formal decision to adopt IAS/IFRS represented a watershed in the long historical development of financialised capitalism in Europe and beyond. It marked the convergence of the EU bloc towards the agency paradigm of corporate governance, stressing the primacy of shareholder value-creation and fiduciary duties (Aglietta and Reberioux, 2005; Horn, 2011; Stout, 2012; Clarke, 2024). As noted by Djelic and Sahlin (2009: 177), this shift represents "a profound redefinition of structuring frames for action and of normative and cognitive reference sets".

Around the year 2000, opposition to global capitalism became increasingly vocal through the alter-globalisation movements. Capturing the essence of this form of exploitative and unsustainable capitalism, Lazonick and Shin (2019) coined the term 'predatory value extraction'. They argue that the success of global multinationals was largely built on extracting value from labour, which wages have not kept up with productivity gains. The authors note that the 'retain-and-reinvest' corporate value regime characteristic of the 1960s–1970s, accompanied by patient capitalism and long-term employment practices, turned into a 'downsize-and-redistribute' system where value is captured by shareholders and managers, while corporations seek to downsize their labour force. During this time, corporate scandals such as Enron and WorldCom, the Asian financial crisis, and growing awareness of the adverse socio-ecological impact of multinationals generated stronger demand for corporate public accountability. In this context, SR regulation re-emerged in the European policy agenda. However, as mentioned, this second wave of SR initiatives was very different from 1970s social accounting. As recalled by an EU official: "There were more demands expressed towards companies but, at the same time, not a willingness to regulate. So the way in between was to ask for transparency, and consumers and investors would judge" (cited in Monciardini and Conaldi, 2019: 247). The contemporary adoption of IFRS standards by the EU, and consequent outsourcing and privatisation of European accounting rules to the IASB, removed the option of unilaterally amending accounting standards to take social and environmental matters into account.

Ideologically, the growing influence of finance-driven accounting within the EU made increasingly inconceivable the prospect of adoption of mandatory SR. In the Commission's jargon (the 2003 EU 'Accounts Modernization Directive'), borrowed from the accounting profession, SR was re-framed as 'non-financial' reporting and defined as a secondary, 'non-binding' business practice, in stark contrast with mandatory financial reporting. Voluntary SR initiatives, such as the GRI, strongly supported by European public authorities (Moon, 2004; Albareda et al., 2008), spread rapidly. Weak and captured SR became a form of 'corporate *noblesse oblige*' (Crouch, 2009), leaving the management of the corporation free to decide whether or not to engage in such practices and how. They effectively served as a legitimising tool for multinationals (Deegan, 2002; Levy et al., 2010), which were facing unprecedented accountability pressures and were seeking a social licence to operate (Djelic and Etchanchu, 2017).

Overall, I maintain that this transformation of SR into a widespread exercise in corporate "impression management" (Cho et al., 2015a) cannot be fully understood without considering the contemporary harmonisation, financialisation, and privatisation of global financial accounting standards (Hopwood, 1994; Botzem and Quack, 2005; Botzem, 2012; Chiapello, 2015). This, in turn, has played a key role in fostering the global spread of a financialised regime of capital accumulation and corporate governance (Jessop 1992 and 2007; Aglietta and Reberioux, 2005; Horn, 2011; Stout, 2012; Clarke, 2024). During this phase, the architecture of financial markets, including financial accounting standards, has become largely independent from national political control (Strange, 1996, 2015). Europe converged towards a privatised and financialised concept of corporate governance, narrowly understood as the problem of making sure that managers (agents) are held accountable to investors (principals) for getting a fair return on their investment (Horn, 2011; Stout, 2012). By excluding other actors (e.g. public authorities, civil society, and organised labour) from questions about corporate control, value creation, and redistribution, this narrow view is at odds with societal corporate accountability and legitimate sustainability goals (McBarnet et al., 2007; Bacq and Aguilera, 2022; Bebbington et al., 2024).

4.3 IFRS Legitimacy Crisis and the Creation of the ISSB

The 2008 financial crisis reduced the neoliberal ideological foundations of business self-regulation and voluntary CSR to ruins, suddenly making apparent the need for a stronger regime of corporate sustainability and accountability.

The global financial crisis revamped discussions about the systemic risks of the current 'casino capitalism' (see Strange 1997; Shaxson 2019) and attracted attention to alternative perspectives on value and valuation, even within mainstream public debates (Mazzucato, 2018; Carney, 2022). More broadly, a combination of complex pluri-crises (e.g. the global financial crisis; climate crisis; the health COVID-19 crisis) contributed to convince political and business leaders of the need for extraordinary measures in response to unprecedented socio-ecological risks (Adams and Abhayawansa, 2022). Conventional economics focused on indefinite growth came to be considered as a major driver of this pluri-crises, provoking climate change and biodiversity loss, affecting people's health and well-being, and increasing inequality (Jackson, 2009; Raworth, 2017; Brand-Correa et al., 2022). A number of economic theories came to be widely discussed in search for alternative paradigms, including post-Keynesian economics, evolutionary economics, ecological economics, and complexity economics (Brand-Correa et al., 2022; Kallis et al., 2025; Parrique, 2025). It is in this context of paradigmatic crisis that a large consensus on the need for profound policy reforms, supporting the sustainability economic transition emerged in Europe. This is evident in von der Leyen's grand speech announcing the adoption of the European Green Deal in which she stated: "Our goal is to reconcile the economy with our planet, to reconcile the way we produce, the way we consume, with our planet and to make it work for our people." Von der Leyen said she was convinced that the old growth model based on fossil fuels and pollution is "out of date and out of touch with our planet", adding "the European Green Deal is our new growth strategy".

Once again, the wider systemic crisis co-evolved with a crisis of the conventional financial accounting paradigm (Burlaud and Colasse, 2011; Adams and Abhayawansa, 2022). In the aftermath of the global financial crisis, privatised and financialised IFRS standards were put into the limelight as a possible contributor to the global financial crisis (Magnan, 2009; Botzem, 2012; Giner and Jorissen, 2020). IAS/IFRS were accused of distorting investors and regulators' perceptions of financial performance and stability, accelerating negative trends that led to the global financial crisis (Magnan, 2009). More broadly, IFRS accounting was associated with more volatile and less conservative financial statements, thus fostering unsustainable short-term-oriented business practices (Adams and Abhayawansa, 2022; Haldane et al, 2024; Mähönen and Palea, 2024). For several years after the financial crisis, there has been a public debate about the opportunity for radical reforms of outdated corporate financial accounting standards and rules (Burlaud & Colasse, 2011; Hoogervorst and Prada, 2015; Giner and Jorissen, 2020; Vollmer, 2024). The publication of the Maystadt report (2013) questioned whether the EU should exert greater political control over the IFRS standard-setting process, prompting changes in the governance structure of EFRAG. In the same time period, one of the main reasons for the EU adoption of IFRS – the convergence of US and European accounting standards – was ended without accomplishing the initial goal (Giner and Jorissen, 2020). By 2018, the IFSR legitimacy crisis became particularly evident when the European Commission issued a consultation document titled "Fitness Check on the EU Framework for Public Reporting by Companies" (European Commission, 2018). The Commission sought comments from "the broadest possible base of stakeholders" to "assess whether the EU reporting framework is still fit for purpose" also in relation to sustainability goals. It includes several instances in which the EU adoption of IFRS is disputed. For instance, in the section "The EU financial reporting framework for listed companies", the document asks whether it is "still appropriate that the IAS Regulation prevents the Commission from modifying the content of IFRS". It also asks whether the EU endorsement process is appropriate to ensure that IFRSs do not pose an obstacle to broader EU policy objectives such as sustainability and long-term investments. Here the answers offered are (a) "By retaining the power to modify the IFRS standards in well-defined circumstances" and (b) "By making explicit in the EU regulatory framework that in order to endorse IFRS that are conducive to the European public good, sustainability and long term investment must be considered".

Building on a conceptualisation widely adopted in EU policy studies, IFRS' legitimacy crisis can be understood through the lens of both input-oriented and output-oriented legitimacy (Scharpf, 1997, 1999). As for accounting standards, input legitimacy refers to the process of standard-setting, considering whether it is inclusive and democratic, adequately taking into account diverse perspectives of stakeholders. Output legitimacy focuses on the effectiveness and results of the standard-setting process, including the usefulness, relevance, and effectiveness of the resulting standards. IFRS adoption can be criticised on the grounds of both types of legitimacy.

On the input legitimacy side, the decision of the EU Commission to adopt IFRS poses two sets of issues. The first concerns the privatisation of standard-setting processes that remain "largely outside the purview of democratic institutions and therefore, liable to questions concerning their legitimacy" (Graz, 2006: 118). As mentioned, IFRS are issued by the International Accounting Standards Board (IASB), a private standard-setter based in London. It is controlled by the IFRS Foundation, a not-for-profit corporation established in Delaware (US), which is financed by powerful industrial and service companies, including large auditing and consulting firms (Botzem, 2012). Concerns have been expressed that EU democratic mechanisms or procedures to link political decisions with citizens' preferences have been effectively weakened, in favour of powerful vested interests (Russell and Dewing, 2007; Palea, 2018; Chiapello & Medjad, 2009; Müller, 2014; Hoogervorst and Prada, 2015). The second concern regards the narrow focus of IFRS on the perspective of financial capital providers (Dillard and Vinnari, 2019). The IASB focus only on financially material disclosure is a major source of legitimacy for a contested shareholder primacy approach to corporate governance and value capture (Gray, 2006; Brown and Dillard, 2015; Birch and Muniese, 2020). This is at odds with the ethos and evolution of corporate sustainability and corporate governance principles (OECD, 2023; see Clarke, 2024), justifying the exclusion of information relevant to other stakeholders from 'what really matters' to corporate executives.

On the output legitimacy side, there is growing evidence that conventional financial accounting is inadequate to explain today's corporate value creation (Deloitte and The Economist Intelligence Unit, 2004; Ocean Tomo, 2020; Friede et al., 2015). There are many, indeed many of them are accountants, who would agree with the authoritative position of Robert Howell, who pointed out on Fortune that "the big three statements – income statement, balance sheet and statement of cash flow – are about as useful as an 80-year-old Los Angeles road map" (see Gazdar 2007:13). This is nothing really new; it has been said for years that the annual report should be remodelled to consider major changes in the way companies operate and value is created and distributed (see e.g. Deegan and Rankin, 1999). However, there has been an understandable resistance from accountants and auditors that see their business thrown into question. For instance, according to a research by Ocean Tomo on the S&P 500 Index (2020), until the 1980s, the traditional annual financial reports used to explain 80 per cent of the market value of a company. Nowadays, they account for less than 20 per cent. While only part of this over 80 per cent value can be captured by looking at ESG data, there is growing consensus that better quality SR could help to address critical gaps in existing financial accounting standards (Friede et al., 2015). As noted by Michael Power, "financial accounting continues to be challenged by conceptual and measurement difficulties in dealing with the rise of the intangible economy and in representing more fluid and hybrid organisational forms" (2018).

As a side-effect of the weakening of financialised capitalism and IFRS legitimacy, demands for mandatory SR regulation re-emerged stronger than ever, not only in the EU but globally. For instance, in a series of widely discussed letters to corporate CEOs, Larry Fink (2020), founder and charismatic leader of BlackRock – the world's largest asset manager, emphatically declared that "Climate change has become a defining factor in companies' long-term prospects. ...I believe we are on the edge of a fundamental reshaping of finance." Fink focuses on the importance of improving accounting for sustainability. "Companies and countries that champion transparency and demonstrate their responsiveness to stakeholders ... will attract investment more effectively, including higher-quality, more patient capital. Important progress improving disclosure has already been made – and many companies already do an exemplary job of integrating and reporting on sustainability – but we need to achieve more widespread and standardized adoption." Fink observations were not dictated by a sudden interest in environmental and societal matters but rather by the rapid growth of European sustainable finance and integration of ESG considerations into mainstream investment (Eccles and Klimenko 2019; Ahlström and Monciardini, 2022). Indeed, according to a global survey, by 2018 more than half of global asset owners were implementing or evaluating ESG considerations in their investment strategy (Ahlström and Monciardini, 2022). Signatories to the UN-backed Principles for Responsible Investment (PRI) jumped from sixty-three investment companies in 2006 with $6.5 trillion in assets under management (AUM) to 1715 signatories in 2018 representing $81.7 trillion in AUM (Eccles and Klimenko, 2019). Given the unprecedented pressure from policymakers and interest of investors in sustainability-related matters, it became increasingly difficult for the IFRS Foundation to justify their choice of ignoring sustainability-related information.

In this context it is possible to understand recent developments in the landscape of SR private standard-setting as an institutional response to the legitimacy crisis of the financial accounting framework. In particular, during this period, such a response has emerged through the creation of two new private standard-setters that stand out because of their significance: IIRC (International Integrated Reporting Council) and the ISSB (International Sustainability Standards Board). Both can be seen as attempts by the accounting profession to control or at least influence the rapid legislative development and harmonisation of SR standards.

The IIRC was created in 2010, in response to the criticism of financial accounting standards emerged during the global financial crisis and it co-evolved with the EU decision to adopt the NFRD (Biondi et al., 2020). Initially, it used such criticism as a source of legitimacy, by framing its mission as an attempt to bring together a variety of stakeholders, including corporations, investors, accountants, but also academics and civil society, to create an 'integrated report' framework or <IRF>. This promised to revolutionise conventional accounting practices to "meet the challenge of communicating value in the 21st Century" (IIRC, 2011). The IIRC had the merit of highlighting some real concerns: (1) "business has become more complex and gaps in traditional reporting have become prominent"; (2) "new reporting requirements have been added through a patchwork of laws, regulations, standards"; (3) "much of the information now provided is disconnected and key disclosure gaps remain" (IIRC, 2011). Notably, they were the same shortcomings that motivated the parallel development of the NFRD by the EU Commision, creating a ambiguous relationship between the two standardisation processes (Biondi et al., 2020). However, a crucial difference between the two standards is that the NFRD adopted a multi-stakeholder approach to SR, while <IRF> was directed to investors, in line with the financialised accounting paradigm (Flower, 2015). Many scholars openly criticised this narrow approach taken by the IIRC for failing sustainability. Milne and Gray (2013: 20) claimed that <IRF> "has virtually nothing – and certainly nothing substantive – to say about either accountability or sustainability". Flower argued that the failure of <IRF> to maintain its original transformative ambition is due to the composition of the IIRC Board. This has been "dominated by the accountancy profession, preparers and regulators ...They outnumbered by far the few representatives of organizations that promoted social and environmental accounting" (Flower, 2015: 2). Eventually, <IRF> failed to become mainstream, because "without regulatory support, it is difficult for a private regulatory standard or framework to be adopted and diffused" (Biondi et al., 2020: 889). However, it influenced the policy and public debate in a crucial period in which the shortcomings of conventional financial accounting were under scrutiny.

Something similar is happening with the establishment, this time directly by the IFRS Foundation, of the ISSB in 2021–2022, arguably in response to growing demands of ESG information from investors and the contemporary appointment of EFRAG as the European standard-setter for SR. As argued by Vollmer (2024: 2), the IFRS Foundation "has been working through new-found sensitivities, questions about what accounting is and who it should be for". Following a public consultation in 2020, the IFRS Foundation claimed that the ISSB could harmonise SR standards by leveraging its expertise in setting accounting standards and use its existing relationships to enforce sustainability reporting (Bohn et al., 2025). The establishment of the ISSB has attracted several critiques. It has been argued that the domains of sustainability and climate are new to the IFRS Foundation, which lacks relevant expertise; SR should be integrated rather than being disclosed separately from the annual report; and the IFRS Foundation could have endorsed already established SR frameworks (Adams and Mueller, 2022; de Villiers et al., 2024; Bohn et al., 2025). The most contested point has been the decision by the ISSB to limit its scope: single (financial) materiality, a narrow focus on investors' information needs, and an interpretation of sustainability as centred only on climate change matters (Abela, 2022; Maechler, 2023; Bohn et al., 2025). Nonetheless, the strong political and corporate network supporting the IFRS Foundation has ensured that the work of the ISSB also received unprecedented recognition and a wide promotion. In particular, it received immediate support from IOSCO (IOSCO, 2023), suggesting that its SR standards may be eventually adopted by companies listed on member stock exchanges (Hummel and Jobst, 2024). It also benefited from the influential support of the so-called 'Big 4' global accounting and auditing firms (Deloitte, PwC, Ernst & Young, and KPMG), which play a significant role both within the ISSB (de Villiers et al., 2024) and in the communication of the new standards towards their corporate clients. What is less clear is the ambivalent relationship between the ISSB, EFRAG and the European Commission. On the one hand, the ISSB contested the work of EFRAG. In particular, ISSB Chair Emmanuel Faber has been very vocal against 'double materiality', the very bone of contention between ISSB and the EU. In an op-ed published by French reference newspaper *Le Monde*, Faber defined it as "an illusion", "seductive, but a trap", "unrealistic", "incompatible with the urgency of the transition", "false hope", "simplistic", and "ineffective" (Faber, 2023). On the other hand, both the ISSB and its network have often emphasised the similarity and convergence between the IFRS S1 and S2 and the ESRS. Indeed they have much publicised the joint publication of an interoperability guidance (EFRAG and IFRS Foundation, 2024). Presenting the guidance, Faber stressed "our deep collaboration with EFRAG", framing the ISSB standards as providing a "global baseline" against which ESRS simply require "incremental disclosures" (EFRAG and IFRS Foundation, 2024).

For the scope of this study, both the IIRC and the ISSB are responses to "developments in the realm of corporate reporting, such as sustainability reporting and non-financial corporate governance reporting" (Hoogervorst and Prada, 2015: 7) that threaten to disrupt the conventional financial accounting paradigm. While they are presented as revolutionary changes, they have the paradoxical effect of placating, appropriating, and incorporating demands for seriously disruptive changes. They followed a similar underlying script: (a) making symbolic concessions to those who pose demands for substantial transformation; and (b) appeasing the momentum and energy for threatening reforms, lowering the pressure on traditional financial accounting to change and adapt to a rapidly evolving context. It is the familiar 'di Lampedusa strategy': "the more things change, the more they stay the same" (Cho et al., 2015b). Drawing on the political theory of Antonio Gramsci, I maintain that the establishment of the ISSB by the IFRS Foundation can be defined as a form of 'transformism' (Gramsci, 1971; Howarth, 2005). That is, growing demands for radical transformations of unsustainable business emerging from a large base of citizens (businessmen, civil society organisations, investors, consumers, etc.) have been disarticulated and captured by incorporating some of their instances (e.g. carbon disclosure) into the conventional accounting practice (i.e. single materiality).

5 Learning from Failure and Success: Proposals for a Paradigmatic Change

Many of the questions that characterise the current SR policy debate are not new. However, they appear more urgent and complex than ever, reflecting broader debates about the limits of economic growth and the role of business in society (Meadows et al. 1972; Streeck, 2011; Jackson, 2009; Raworth, 2017; Kallis et al., 2025). What is the purpose of large corporations? What sort of 'value' companies generate? Is it only 'economic' value? Is it only shareholder value? How do companies impact the social environment in which they operate? Should conventional accounting be radically transformed to include sustainability-related information? How financial and sustainability disclosure could be better integrated? To whom companies and their managers should be held accountable? What is the role of private standard-setting bodies? What is the purpose of accounting standards? What is the role of public authorities and lawmakers? While some of these questions go back to the corporate governance debates of the 1930s and the 1970s, there are key differences. Back then, regulatory initiatives were politically and legislative-driven. Nowadays, most accounting and business regulatory initiatives are transnational, privatised, and market-driven.

Certainly, over the past fifteen years, we have witnessed a deep legitimacy crisis of the financialised global economic model, dominated by speculative rather than productive activities (Mazzucato, 2018; Lazonick and Shin, 2019). As discussed, short-terminism and shareholder-centred corporate governance as well as accounting standards only focused on financial information and on the needs of financial capital providers have come under unprecedented scrutiny. And yet, as already noted by Botzem (2012: 15), it is remarkable how international accounting standards, despite open criticism, have weathered the storm brought about by the financial crisis and managed to maintain the status quo. European SR reforms have emerged in isolation from questions about financial accounting reforms, leaving the shareholder-centric approach and unusual privatised governance of the IASB's untouched.

As argued by Ahlström and Monciardini (2022: 193–194), at the heart of the mix of undeniable success and structural shortcomings that characterises the ongoing third wave of SR regulation is a glaring paradox. On the one hand,

> during the period 2009–2019, the so-called 'sustainable finance' has come to play a key role in mobilising the necessary capital to deliver on crucial EU sustainability policy objectives. ... On the other hand, the increasing importance of financial markets, institutions and motives in the world economy – often called financialisation (Epstein, 2005) – has been frequently identified as one of the main root causes of our unprecedented social and environmental problems. (Fletcher 2012; Büscher et al. 2014)

Thus, the authors underline the importance of unpacking the paradoxical nature of the current relationship between finance and sustainability (see also Yan et al., 2019). The financial logic could simultaneously aid and constrain the success of sustainability reforms: finance as a source of legitimate ends constrains the social and environmental motivations for sustainability reforms; at the same time, finance as a provider of means supplies the societal resources to establish successful sustainability reforms. From a theoretical perspective, a possible way forward indicated by Yan and colleagues (2019) in order to make sense of the contradictions and ambiguity of '(un)sustainable finance', which applies also to SR, is to distinguish between the end goals towards which actors should be directed – what I call the 'constitutional' sustainability principles (Kampourakis, 2018; Herlin-Karnell, 2023; Groppi, 2023) – and the means by which these ends are to be achieved – finance and the financial logic. This useful articulation between means and goals is common practice in the literature on institutional logics that also warns against the risks of 'means-ends decoupling' (see Wijen, 2014). This concept describes situations where, in response to institutional pressures, organisations engage in activities that are weakly linked to their goals and turn out to be largely ineffective (Bromley and Powell, 2012; Wijen, 2014). The recent backlash against corporate sustainability and the reaction of national and EU policy-makers is only the latest case of 'means-ends' decoupling in the history of European SR.

I agree with Andreas Rasche and Georg Kell (2025) that the EU "based its desire to simplify on a misleading narrative; a narrative that sees reporting and due diligence as a cost burden which undercuts competitiveness". Finding a new narrative means, above all, moving from the dominant 'cost narrative', that is, sustainability as a burden, to a 'value narrative', which re-connects corporate sustainability and accountability regulation to its intended purpose, users, and beneficiaries. Contributing to this timely and crucial public debate, the following pages briefly outline a series of proposals for a paradigmatic change in corporate reporting. While they focus on the EU policy debate, they could be considered by public authorities from different latitudes in order to strengthen their regulatory approach. In line with other analyses (de Bakker et al., 2020), I believe that the lack of vision of the regulator comes from a cognitive capture – a situation in which the regulator begins to think like the regulated actors (Carpenter and Moss, 2014). Thus, the rationale behind our proposals is that the needed changes shall not be merely based on technical regulatory solutions. They require above all deep changes in the underlying normative discourse and regulatory mindset used to think about sustainability, corporate reporting, and its regulation.

5.1 Sustainability Is the Overarching Constitutional Principle, Not Just a Set of Issues to Be Added to the Annual Report

Too often the policy and regulatory debate on SR has been framed in terms of reporting on financial *plus* sustainability information (thus the expression 'non-financial' information in the NFRD) – then questioning what is the best way of framing the relationship between the two. Drawing on the history of European attempts to regulate SR (Sections 3 and 4), one can identify four narratives through which policymakers can (and did) look at the possible relationships between financial reporting and sustainability-related matters (Figure 3).

From the 1980s until the 2008 global financial crisis, the prevailing narrative has been that '*this is not accounting*', drawing a line between socio-ecological and financial matters, as illustrated by the widely used distinction between "financial" and "non-financial" reporting. While disdain for 'narrative', 'boilerplate' SR disclosure is still present in part of the accounting profession and standard-setters (Wagenhofer, 2024), this view has lost currency, particularly because of demands for high-quality ESG information by investors. Already the

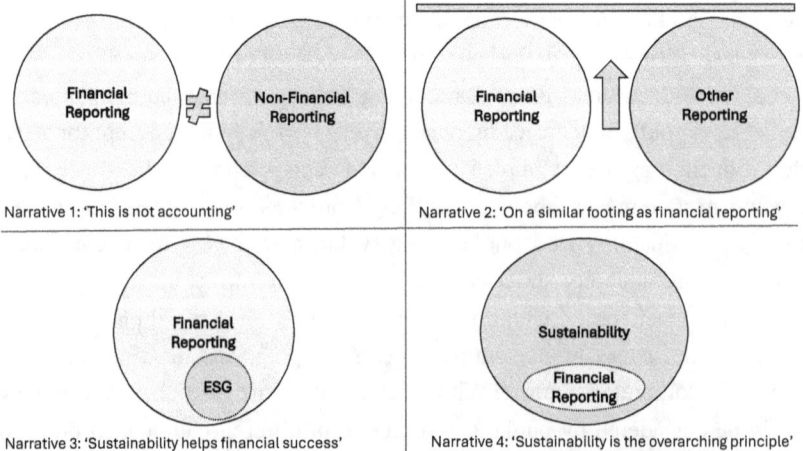

Figure 3 Four narratives defining the relationship between financial reporting and sustainability

NFRD and, in particular, the CSRD are underpinned by a second narrative, which frames extant financial reporting practices as the golden standard to which SR can be added as a second pillar. Thus, frequent expressions in the current EU policy circles stating that "improved depth and quality of reporting can only be realized when financial and sustainability reporting are on an *equal footing*" (GRI, 2020); and "[f]or the first time ever, sustainability reporting will be on an *equal footing* with financial reporting" (European Commission, 2022). I believe this narrative might have been helpful to legitimise SR with business actors and accounting professionals (Etzion and Ferraro, 2010). However, it is also a dangerous narrative, because (a) it implies that current IFRS financial accounting standards are fine as they are, preventing them from changing; (b) it re-produces the distinction financial/non-financial reporting in the form of financial/other reporting, preventing business information from being analysed more holistically, adopting an integrated perspective; (c) it doubles corporate reporting efforts, generating questions about the significant cost of additional SR data collection. Currently, this arbitrary distinction between reporting practices appears increasingly untenable. As SR becomes increasingly a legal requirement, corporate actors increasingly demand for some form of streamlining and integration. The CSRD's requirement to include SR into the annual report, side by side with the financial statements, is accelerating this process. Thus, a third narrative has come to dominate the EU policy debate: '*sustainability helps financial success.*' Therefore, ESG disclosure – that is, financially material sustainability-related information – has to be seen as part and parcel of the corporate financial communication to financial capital providers. Many influential SR standard-setters fall within this narrative, such as the Task Force on Climate-related Financial Disclosures (TCFD), Climate Disclosure Standards Board (CDSB), Sustainability Accounting Standards Board (SASB), International Integrated Reporting Council (IIRC), and the International Sustainability Standards Board (ISSB). This narrative can be helpful to dismiss attempts to deregulate EU accountability rules, by underlining the relevance of SR from an investor perspective. However, I will argue that this is also a limited and rather short-sighted approach, because it subsumes sustainability disclosure to a financial materiality test. Its distortive effect is that corporate sustainability initiatives that fail to deliver financial value come to be seen as patently unsustainable, no matter their social and environmental benefits (Buller, 2022; Archer, 2024).

Contributing to a new post-Omnibus narrative (Rasche and Kell, 2025), I advance a fourth possible narrative. I contend that sustainability is not just a set of datapoints to be added or included into the annual report but *the overarching normative principle* that applies to corporate reporting as a whole, including financial accounting. Indeed, according to some prominent legal scholars, it is already possible to identify sustainability as an overarching constitutional objective of the European Treaties, which has yet to "trickle down" into all aspects of EU company law and securities law (Sjåfjell and Wiesbrock, 2015; Mähönen and Palea, 2024). This is in line with approaches to corporate governance that argue for the fiduciary duty of corporate's executives to respect human rights or aligning corporate strategies to the societal objective of combating climate change (Stout, 2012; McPhail et al., 2016; Clarke, 2024). Such constitutional approach to SR is based on a number of legal and normative sources (Kampourakis, 2018; Herlin-Karnell, 2023; Groppi, 2023), including the recognition of the fundamental right to a healthy environment as well as a growing trend towards constitutional environmentalism. Unlike the market-driven narrative that 'sustainability helps financial success', this approach essentially re-publicises accounting standards. It reaffirms accounting as a political economic tool aimed at achieving public policy objectives. In fact, it suggests prioritising public health goals, including human well-being and environmental growth, over measuring performance only on financial success.

In this sense, the approach taken by the EU so far is inadequate. Taking sustainability goals seriously would require systematically reviewing accounting rules based on their compatibility with the broader EU and national fundamental objectives of creating a more circular, just, and low-carbon economy (Sjåfjell and Bruner, 2019). An emergent stream of academic papers seems to support this claim. For instance, Scholten, Lambooy, Renes, and Bartels illustrate (2020) how the International Financial Reporting Standards (IFRS) accounting framework does not encourage corporate climate change disclosure, advantaging non-renewable energy as compared to renewable energy companies. Haldane, Migliavacca, and Palea (2024) demonstrate that there is a relationship between changes in accounting rules – the adoption of IFRS fair value accounting – and increasing short-termism in company management. The authors argue that this is leading to underinvestment in the real economy and particularly in the transition to a more just and greener economic model.

5.2 Overcome the Institutional Analogy between Financial Accountancy and Reporting for Social and Environmental Impact

As mentioned in Section 3, for many years SR has been a voluntary practice and, as such, it struggled immensely to be accepted and recognised by business organisations. As illustrated by the work of Etzion and Ferraro (2010), in order to legitimise this new practice in the eyes of business executives, in the 1990s voluntary social and environmental disclosure came to be structured as analogous to existing financial accounting practices. As discussed by a large body of literature, the analogy in argumentation plays a key role in both social and natural sciences and the promotion and shaping of institutional design (Hesse, 1963; Lawrence et al., 2002). In this sense, the development of SR has been conceptually constructed largely through this analogy, in terms of similarity or departure from the financial accounting discourse and institutions. As noted by Archer (2024), "financial reporting comes to be implicitly seen as the golden standard for nonfinancial reporting". For instance, the GRI, the SASB, the IIRC, the EFRAG, and the ISSB are structured similarly to financial accounting standard-setting bodies such as the IASB. They often employ or are led by trained accountants, and sustainability matters are presented in a way that mimics financial reporting as a form of business communication for financial actors and other stakeholders to understand the social and environmental performance of a company.

The analogy with financial reporting provides a distinct rationale for regulating SR centred on the assumption that markets, equipped with accurate data about social and environmental impacts, will lead to efficient and optimal solutions, such as offsetting pollution via investments in pollution mitigation (Archer, 2024). Notwithstanding the crucial theoretical and practical contribution of the accounting profession, I argue that IFRS (i.e. shareholder-driven financial reporting) is not the golden standard to follow, rather a model to overcome. This analogy has limited the inputs of other forms of expertise, particularly relevant to the development of SR regulation. For instance, it is fair to say that financial accountants and auditors lack the necessary understanding of issues such as climate change, human rights violations, circular economy, and biodiversity. As sustainability requires a multidisciplinary effort, it would be crucial to have much greater input from outside accounting and finance expertise. Indeed, the most radical and innovative developments in SR come from bending, blending, and hybridising accounting practices with other expertise (see Miller, 1998; Hopwood, 2007; Vollmer, 2024), such as the cases of accounting for circularity, double materiality, and human rights due diligence (McPhail et al., 2016; Arjaliès et al., 2023; Vollmer, 2024). However, much of this work has been developed in isolation from mainstream accounting discourses due to a 'silo mentality' of policymakers and practitioners (Unerman et al., 2018; Vollmer, 2024).

More needs to be done to integrate this broader body of knowledge into the regulatory debate about accounting for sustainability. The key is to turn it into an opportunity for mutual learning and cross-fertilisation rather than a 'turf war' between competing professional claims (Monciardini, 2016). As argued by Vollmer (2024: 12): "It is hard to avoid the impression that the established institutions of the profession continue to imagine the core of accounting expertise as firmly settled in a single-materiality, business-entity and assets-worried understanding of what matters ...." Building on Vollmer's conceptualisation (2024), a new narrative for SR regulation requires a better understanding and integration of three 'spheres' of expertise: the market-driven financial accounting sphere, which is dominant among business and policymakers (Barker, 2025), the public sphere and the ecosphere (see Figure 4). They have developed SR practices largely in isolation, underpinned by alternative bodies of knowledge and justifications for mandatory SR.

As mentioned throughout this work, the *sphere of financial accounting* has been developed in a close and mutually constitutive relationship with the financialisation of the economic order (Hopwood, 1992; Plantin et al., 2008; Miller and Power, 2013). Thus, it relates to processes of 'economisation' (Polanyi, 1944) and, more specifically, 'assetisation', that is, turning nature into financial assets (Birch and Muniesa, 2020; Buller, 2022; Archer, 2024). According to this perspective, financial markets serve as 'the' reference point for valuing an asset. Another implication of the financial accounting perspective is to define organisational boundaries according to a narrow theory of the firm

Figure 4 Extending accounting for sustainability beyond Anglo-Saxon financial accounting

(Palea, 2018, 2022), based on transaction cost economics (Williamson, 1981, 1985). This reduces SR to an atomistic representation of organisational practices, detached from large economic, societal, and ecological questions. However, the field of economics is going through a profound transformation, moving beyond the neoclassical paradigm (Jackson, 2009; Raworth, 2017; Brand-Correa et al., 2022; Kallis et al., 2025). New economic theories, such as 'ecological economics' (Kallis et al., 2025; Parrique, 2025), are focused on improving human well-being, focusing on a regenerative and redistributive economy. They have been an important source of inspiration for a paradigmatic change also in corporate reporting (Adams and Abhayawansa, 2022; Bebbington et al., 2020 and 2024).

The *public sphere* can be defined as a social space where financial reporting encounters public accountability; therefore, it "tends to be where accounts go after accountants are done with them" (Vollmer, 2024: 7). Here SR has been mainly developed and rationalised as a means towards corporate democracy and societal accountability, driven chiefly by the growing activism of Civil Society Organisations (CSOs), like Amnesty International or Greenpeace, against corporate abuses. As noted by Gray (2010: 550), "Enquiry into social accounting offers, inter alia, the promise (however idealized) of an international corporate, institutional and financial complex held substantially accountable to civil society for its activities." According to this public accountability rationale, mandatory SR is justified by the democratic principle of 'rights to information' about the impact of corporations on society and the environment – rights which derive from a number of sources: legal, quasi-legal, moral, and so on (see McBarnet et al., 2007). Here mandatory SR is not derived from market demand but part of a global trend towards corporate sustainability and accountability laws (Sjåfjell, 2024). In Europe, this trend is reflected in many legislative initiatives such as the French Law Devoir de Vigilance, the EU CSDDD, but also the Ecodesign for Sustainable Products Regulation (ESPR) and EU Sustainable Corporate Governance (European Commission, 2020). The public sphere is a source of re-publicisation and re-politicisation of privatised accounting standards, often seen as "a source of trouble and cause of concern for accountants" (Vollmer, 2024: 7). In fact, it questions the legitimacy of conventional reporting practices (Guthrie and Parker, 1989; Deegan, 2002). For instance, it criticises SR as a "façade" (Biondi et al., 2020), a form of "organised hypocrisy" (Cho et al., 2015a) or the IASB for lacking democratic accountability (Chiapello and Medjad, 2009). More broadly, it raises questions about the legitimacy of an economic regime as a whole. For instance, such a perspective might lead to question why financial capital providers have a dominant role in EU accounting laws (Owen et al., 2000; Stout, 2012; Palea, 2018).

However, much of the current momentum for regulating SR comes from the *ecosphere*, justified by the ecological imperative to act now to avoid the dire consequences for humanity of the transgression of planetary boundaries and critical "tipping points" (Lenton et al., 2019). This science-based body of knowledge is hybridising financial accounting with corporate sustainability metrics. Ever more often SR requires to include KPIs such as: CO_2 emissions reduction in kt, energy consumption in kWh, water usage in metric tonnes, waste reduction in cubic metres, plastic reduction in metric tonnes, material efficiency in material input per unit of service (MIPS), compliance with chemical safety requirements, and so on. Examples of SR regulation that stem from this sphere include the Eco-Management and Audit Scheme (EMAS), and the Science Based Target initiative (SBTi): the UN Sustainable Development Performance Indicators (SDPI). Another example is the EU Sustainable Finance Taxonomy, which ought to be 'technical' and 'science-based'. Underpinned by the currency of science in our modern society (Bothello and Djelic-Salles, 2018; Tilsted et al., 2023), sustainability metrics are increasingly deployed for environmental management and accurate monitoring of corporate impacts. Yet, this approach remains quite remote and rather disconnected from the conventional horizon of accounting standards. It generates questions about the adequacy of the conventional financial accounting paradigm and the expertise of trained accountants (Bebbington et al., 2020; Haldane et al., 2024). Hardyment effectively expresses the scientific legitimacy tensions between financial accounting and the ecosphere as he argues: It's become fashionable to claim that sustainability fits easily with finance. That's only partially true. . . . With sustainability, our field of vision is wider. The boundaries stretch beyond the factory gates and office walls. . . . Financial accounting draws a thick line around the business entity. But sustainability impacts and dependencies span suppliers, distributors, customers, consumers, communities and end of product life. The systemic nature is what makes them so challenging to measure. (2024: 121–122). On the other side, valuation tensions might emerge between technocentric, science-based metrics and the sphere of public accountability. Devising suitable SR metrics is never merely a technical exercise. It requires making normative and political choices. As Hardyment (2024: 147–148) puts it, the problem is that most sustainability matters, and particularly social matters, are complex phenomena expressed into abstract, multifaceted ideas that require judgement, making them "fiendishly hard to standardise" in the same way as emissions or waste.

I argue that the relationship between these three spheres of SR regulation remains poorly conceptualised. This is generating tensions and misalignments in our understanding of SR regulation that require greater scholarly attention.

5.3 Double Materiality Is Not a 'Double Vision', but a 'Join the Dots' Activity Providing a Fuller Picture

The conventional approach to business reporting – including SR – has been company-centric (i.e. the 'true and fair view' doctrine), following the legal-ownership conventional organisational boundaries linked to transaction costs (Hopwood, 1983). However, this perspective has often been challenged by advocates of social and environmental reporting as too narrowly focused on value creation for the organisation and its shareholders, rather than shared value for society and environmental protection (Klettner et al., 2014; Magnan and Michelon, 2024; Barker and Mayer, 2024). Over time this ambiguity has created two ideas of the materiality assessment that the EU policymakers seem to struggle to reconcile (Raith, 2023). On the one hand, the 'true and fair view' perspective, centred on the financial success of the reporting business entity, typical of the financial accounting tradition. This financial materiality perspective is centred on the privileged relationship with an investor type of audience. On the other hand, the socio-ecological perspective, focused on the impact of corporate activities on society and nature. This broader perspective focuses on externalities and the social licence of business to operate, and the corporate obligations towards stakeholders, society, and nature.

The concept of 'double materiality assessment' (DMA), introduced by the NFRD and then fully established in the CSRD, seemed to finally redraw the conventional boundaries of corporate reporting, overcoming this harmful dualism between corporate and socio-ecological objectives. The DMA is the cornerstone of the EU approach to SR, requiring "undertakings to report both on the impacts of the activities of the undertaking on people and the environment, and on how sustainability matters affect the undertaking" (CSRD para 29). The two perspectives – often called 'inside-out' and 'outside-in' – are clearly complementary and intertwined views, helping companies to reflect on their relationship with the external environment in which they operate. Therefore, DMA could offer the opportunity for the design of new and integrated approaches (see Section 5.1). It could also contribute to decoupling social and environmental reporting from the analogy with traditional financial accounting (see Section 5.2), highlighting the need for adopting new methodologies and expertise. As maintained by Vollmer (2024: 2), in this "moment of vacillation between a fundamental course-correction and a mere wobble", the definition of what is 'material' is at the core of current debates "about accounting's place and purpose". Indeed, the introduction of DMA is considered as a radical innovation in the sphere of financial accounting. It represents an "apparent deviation from the European Commission's previous approach of expanding the interpretation of 'financial materiality' and confining the intended audience to investors" (Abhayawansa, 2022: 1372).

However, I contend that the definition of DMA contained in the CSRD was quite ambiguous and its operationalisation in the ESRS is disappointing and confusing, considerably reducing its transformative potential. EFRAG was tasked to further specify the DMA concept. Arguably, it failed the test because there is evidence that companies demand for more guidance on the application of the DMA and, post-Omnibus, the Commission (2025) required EFRAG to "provide clearer instructions on how to apply the materiality principle". While critics of the DMA would argue that this is a fundamentally flawed concept (Faber, 2023; Barkerand Mayer, 2024), I rather argue that the DMA has been poorly constructed and communicated. In the CSRD the word 'financial materiality' is never mentioned. Yet, in the ESRS it quietly and gradually appears – based on the existing IFRS definition of financial materiality – alongside 'impact materiality'. The result is that EFRAG is simply reproducing the harmful dualism between "investors" and "nature" (Barker and Mayer, 2024) that plagued SR public debates over the last four decades. This allowed many to criticise the EU approach to materiality as confusing and ineffective. Barker and Mayer (2024) are comparing the DMA adopted by EFRAG to a "double vision", meaning that it forces companies to try to look at their strategies, impacts, risks, and opportunities through two rather different lenses: financial success or socio-ecological impact. Since the relationship between the two lenses is poorly explained, ultimately EFRAG is leaving wide latitude to business organisations and influential market actors to fill in the details that ESRS have left ambiguous (Edelman, 2016; Maher et al., 2020). Ultimately, this 'double vision' – investors and nature – suggests a separation between two realities and it is likely to reproduce the old habit of turning impact materiality into a "façade" (Biondi et al., 2020), a form of "organised hypocrisy" (Cho et al., 2015a).

Moving from the premise that accounting is "a metaphorical enterprise" (Morgan, 1986: 480; also Edgley, 2014) and "as such it mobilises a wide range of metaphors" (Vollmer, 2024: 2), I would rather suggest that the DMA is like a 'joining the dots' activity, providing a more complete, granular, and updated picture of the company in its broader context. This act of putting together the company's full image, indivisible from the company's environment, can be a powerful metaphor to explain the essence of the DMA experience. Thus, the DMA is not as the result of "seeing double" (Barker and Mayer, 2024), rather as the result of the company's act of looking at itself as part of the context in which it operates. Some important characteristics emerge from this alternative metaphor. First of all, given that practically every firm is part of someone else's value chain, the DMA provides a fuller, much more complete, picture of the reporting entity because it shows its networked organisation and interdependencies with suppliers, other stakeholders, and with the socio-ecological context. This alone represents a shift in the mindset of companies that aims to address the shortcomings of the conventional "restrictive view" (Zambon, 2002: 26) of current financial accounting practices. This leads to the second characteristic: the DMA is an objective exercise. Here the approach to materiality adopted by the CSRD differs from both the GRI and the IFRS Foundation. Its peculiarity is a search for greater *objectivity* in assessing the firm's position in the environment in which it operates. Rather than being based on selective stakeholder perspectives (GRI) or on the perspective of a hypothetical investor (IFRS), the CSRD draws materiality on a thorough assessment of the actual positive and negative impact of corporate actions. Thirdly, DMA is an integrative, holistic exercise. Particularly through the due diligence process, it provides an opportunity to the whole company and, above all, to the corporate executives and the board, to learn a great deal about the organisation itself. Preliminary feedback from companies reporting under the CSRD already suggest that this is leading to a better integration of different functions and understanding of the organisation as a whole (PwC, 2024; WAE and HEC, 2025).

By departing DMA from existing financial and/or impact materiality practices, standard-setters could really transform conventional SR. Here, the key is to remember that SR "should be a natural extension of action ... It is this relationship that turns the costs of reporting into an investment in effective risk management" (Shift, 2023). For instance, the disclosure of information about the socio-ecological impact of corporations can be based on innovative forms of inter-organisational accounting (Carlsson-Wall et al., 2018) that could help foster regenerative and sustainable circular ecosystems (Aarikka-Stenroos et al., 2021; Monciardini et al., 2024). Similarly, one could think about new ways to share industry-wide corporate accountability information (e.g. disclosure on issues such as modern slavery in a given supply chain) and sustainability best practices. As such, DMA could cut costs and favour cross-sector, pre-competitive, collaborations focused on addressing a shared societal issue or sustainability challenge. Reporting and verification could be increasingly seen as a public policy instrument of governance of corporations: the last phase of an ongoing collective due diligence process.

5.4 Connectivity of Reporting Reforms with the Other EU Sustainability Law Initiatives

While the EU approach to SR is strongly linked to the EU sustainable finance initiative – as often highlighted by the EU Commission – it is poorly connected to other relevant EU regulatory initiatives (see Mélon, 2026). An example of this disconnection concerns the poor consideration given so far in the debate on the EU regulation of SR to pre-existing EU environmental management, reporting, and audit schemes. As discussed in Section 3.2, during the early 2000s the EU Commission had developed and tested a number of methodologies and initiatives, such as the EU Ecolabel Product Environmental Footprint and Organisation Environmental Footprint methods, elaborated as a common way of measuring the environmental performance of business organisations (Iraldo and Barberio, 2017; Bach et al., 2018). In particular, it is worth mentioning the EU Eco-Management and Audit Scheme (EMAS). In fact, already in 2002, an EU CSR Communication called for examining whether EMAS could be extended to the management of social performance (European Commission, 2009). Building on the extensive experience of EMAS to develop the European sustainability reporting standards would have helped to provide comparable and relevant information and connect the NFRD and the CSRD with the aim of creating a European circular economy (European Commission, 2017b). There is also empirical evidence of the positive effects on the behaviour and corporate sustainability performance of EMAS-registered companies (Heinelt, 2019). Nonetheless, this option has been discarded in favour of financial accounting-like and market-driven reporting frameworks developed by EFRAG, a body with limited expertise on sustainability issues.

Originally, the CSRD was conceived as a major piece of a broader tectonic shift in the EU economy and society (Kourula et al., 2019; Sjåfjell, 2024). In fact, I would argue that this directive is related to all the objectives of the Green Deal: decarbonisation, resource-efficiency, competitiveness, protecting the health and well-being of citizens, decoupling economic growth from resource use, a just transition, growth, and sustainable investment. However, rather than adopting a broader system thinking approach to the sustainability transition, using SR as a leverage for a new political economic strategy, the EU has opted for a narrower, depoliticised view. That is, SR is needed as part of the EU action plan facilitating sustainable finance Thus, it has a close relationship with other important legislative measures that govern financial disclosure, in particular, the Taxonomy Regulation (concerned with the sustainability of economic activities) and the Sustainable Finance Disclosure Regulation (focused on the sustainability of financial products) (see Hummel and Jobst, 2024: 331). However, much more could be done to link reporting practices to a broader range of public policies. CSRD rules could be better integrated across a wide range of regulatory-driven developments (e.g. critical raw materials, battery regulation, deforestation, etc.) to encourage organisational change and avoid unnecessary administrative burden (see Deloitte, 2024; Mélon, 2026). A case in point, ESRS 5 requires companies to report on resources use and circular economy action plans. EFRAG's work could have been linked more clearly to other circularity policy initiatives, such as the digital product passport (DPP). DPP is a new EU regulation, part of the Ecodesign for Sustainable Products Regulation, requiring nearly all products sold in the EU to offer a detailed digital record of a product's lifecycle, including emission footprint, raw material sourcing, and supplier information (European Union, 2024).

In particular, the CSRD was closely related to another much debated Green Deal measure, the Sustainable Corporate Governance Initiative (SCGI). In 2020, the first draft of the SCGI gained global attention, mainly because it proposed to overcome a shareholder-centric approach to corporate governance. The draft requires (or allows) company directors to take into account all stakeholders' interests, as part of their duty of care to promote the company's interest and objectives (European Commission, 2020). It also refers to enabling companies to focus on "long-term sustainable value creation" (Sjåfjell, 2024). Moreover, as part of the SCGI, the Commission committed to introducing rules for mandatory CSDDD. However, the SCGI met extraordinary business opposition. The Commission soon took a step back in terms of reforming directors' duties, the term 'sustainable value creation' disappeared from the table, while the 2022 CSDDD proposal experienced a rocky road towards adoption in 2024, with several rounds of push back (Sjåfjell, 2024; Bueno et al., 2024). As mentioned, due to the Omnibus proposal, at the moment of completing this work (May 2025) there is a real risk that the CSDDD will never be implemented (Leali et al., 2025). Without a comprehensive corporate governance reform and a strong sustainability due diligence process, the effectiveness of mandatory SR has been abated. Nowadays, the paradoxical situation is that ESRS 1 explicitly states that due diligence "informs the undertaking's assessment of its material impacts, risks and opportunities". And yet, it also adds "ESRS do not impose any conduct requirements in relation to due diligence; nor do they extend or modify the role of the administrative, management or supervisory bodies of the undertaking with regard to the conduct of due diligence".

5.5 Extend the Capacity and Coordination of the Users of Sustainability Reporting

This work has demonstrated that attempts to regulate SR have repeatedly failed to deliver on initial high expectations and EU regulators are, once again, at risk of being captured by the regulatory targets (the issuers of SR). Thus, urgent questions remain about the credibility of public authorities in delivering an adequate level of sustainability-related information that can meet the needs of the intended users of such information. In other words, it is worth questioning how we can avoid another regulatory failure.

Drawing on business accountability regulation and governance studies (Abbott et al., 2017; Koenig-Archibugi and Macdonald, 2017; Monciardini and Conaldi, 2019; Brès et al., 2019), I suggest that this crucial question can be addressed by considering the asymmetry between the 'supply-side' and the 'demand-side' of SR regulation. This is illustrated in Figure 5, elaborated from Monciardini and Conaldi (2019). It shows that the conventional understanding of SR regulation is reduced to a two-party relationship between rulemakers (R), such as the European Commission, and rule-takers (T), that is, the preparers of SR. In effect, a recurring element that has emerged from reviewing the long history of SR regulation is that every time there is a momentum for mandatory SR, there are frequent references to the beneficiaries (B): for example, "the current level of transparency in this field" is "unable to meet their needs" (European Commission, 2013). However, beneficiaries tend to disappear from the EU regulatory debate when there is a regulatory capture (e.g. in 2004 when the CSR multi-stakeholder approach failed) or when there is a backlash (e.g. the Omnibus regulatory U-turn). This has been evident when, in February 2025, the Commission decided to adopt fast-track procedure, inviting a majority of corporations for consultations about the future of the CSRD, CSDDD, and the Taxonomy. According to CSOs (FoE, 2025), some of these companies were taken to court for violating human rights or are oil and gas companies. "Victims of corporate abuse, workers in exploitative supply chains, and frontline communities are not consulted on the Omnibus – but corporations are" (ECCJ, 2025). Significantly, beneficiaries such as investors, expressing a keen interest in SR, and other intended users of such information were not invited (UNPRI, IIGCC, Eurosif, 2025). Figure 5 also illustrates the major role and influence of regulatory intermediaries (I), such as consultants, accountants, and auditors, but also ESG analysts. They can influence what rules are enacted, in whose interest they are made, and how these rules are interpreted and implemented.

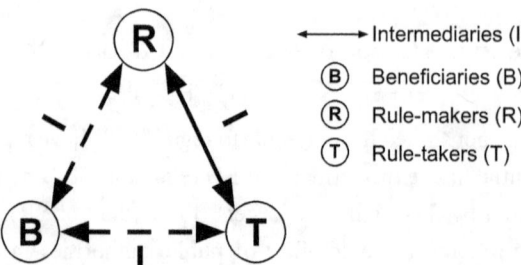

Figure 5 Weak and divided beneficiaries explain SR regulatory capture

By juxtaposing the supply-side (T) and demand-side (B) for SR regulation, this conceptualisation has the merit of clearly highlighting the need for "stronger and better-coordinated beneficiaries' intermediaries in order to achieve more effective corporate conduct regulation" (Monciardini and Conaldi, 2019: 240). Indeed, many proponents of 'stakeholder democracy' (Matten and Crane, 2005) or 'deliberative democracy' (Scherer and Palazzo, 2008) tend to take for granted the capacity of corporate stakeholders to fill the "democracy gap and make corporate decisions more accountable" (Scherer and Palazzo 2011: 912). For historical reasons, explored elsewhere (see Monciardini and Conaldi, 2019; Djelic and Etchanchu, 2017) and related to the global expansion of business operations and the emphasis on shareholders' primacy, SR beneficiaries are fragmented between financial and social stakeholders, increasingly virtualised and dispersed groups of actors that struggle to collaborate and influence the SR regulatory process. As argued by Cooper and Owen, the prevailing approach to SR reporting did fail "to address the issue of effective utilization of information by recipients, and associated power differentials ... if accountability is to be achieved stakeholders need to be empowered" (2007: 653). Similarly, Greenwood and Kamoche (2013) warn that deficient stakeholder involvement renders social auditing ineffective. On the other hand, as explained throughout this contribution, the supply side and its intermediaries – that is, accountants and auditors paid by the firms – strongly influence the SR regulatory process (Perry and Nölke, 2006; Botzem, 2012). For instance, Fransen and LeBaron (2019) unearth evidence that supposedly 'independent' intermediaries (e.g. professional accountants and auditors) construct weak social auditing standards and reporting frameworks that are used by companies as a self-referential and legitimising tool (see also Milne and Gray, 2013; LeBaron et al., 2017).

As noted by Monciardini and Conaldi (2019), this 'neutralisation of beneficiaries' is particularly problematic because accountability regulation, such as SR standards, works indirectly and requires active beneficiaries to be effective. SR increases "the flow of information to the parties affected by corporate activity, other market actors, and civil society groups, who may then rely on this information, for example, in deciding whether to buy the company's products or to mount a media campaign against it" (Parkinson, 1996: 18). This indirect regulatory mechanism ought to raise the reputational cost of corporate irresponsibility while rewarding responsible companies. However, if the information is not used or useful or – crucially – if SR users and beneficiaries simply do not have the organisational capabilities to hold corporations accountable, the effect on corporate conduct is very limited. Then, SR might simply become a legitimising tool for corporate irresponsibility and greenwashing, a form of "impression management" (Dey 2003; Cho et al., 2012).

I maintain that governments and public authorities should start seeing themselves as primary users of SR, together with investors and CSOs, thus strengthening the 'demand-side'. If the previous waves of sustainability reporting standardisation have been driven by the information needs of organised labour (1970s), CSOs (2000s), and responsible investors (2010s), future reforms should be driven by the government's need for information useful to monitor and compare corporate actions on issues such as carbon emissions, inequality in the workplace, widespread human rights violations, and corruption. The development of a society-centred DMA outlined in Section 5.3) should primarily be used by governments to establish whether companies meet minimum standards associated with changing societal expectations – the so-called "social licence to operate" (Hall and Jeanneret, 2015). Companies should be pushed towards improving their performance – as EMAS does for environmental performance – against a limited set of clear criteria, and they should face greater scrutiny if they consistently underperform. At the same time, sustainability information has to be taken into account to reward companies that are creating shared value, for instance through tax breaks and by integrating this information in the emerging green and sustainable procurement frameworks of public sector organisations. As happens with EMAS in certain European Member States, the EU Commission should also seriously consider the possibility of providing financial incentives to help business organisations cover the substantial costs of properly collecting, reporting, and externally validating sustainability information (Iraldo et al., 2009; Heinelt, 2019). Equally, one should require full disclosure from the governments themselves that will lead by example and embed a reformed framework for sustainability reporting in their own operations.

Abbreviations

CSOs	Civil Society Organisations
CSR	Corporate social responsibility
CSDDD	Corporate Sustainability Due Diligence Directive
CSRD	Corporate Sustainability Reporting Directive
DD	Due diligence
EU	European Union
ECB	European Central Bank
EMAS	Eco-Management and Audit Scheme
ESPR	Ecodesign for sustainable products regulation
EFRAG	European Financial Reporting Advisory Group
ESG	Environmental, social and governance
ESRS	European sustainability reporting standards
IASB	International Accounting Standards Board
IFRS	International financial reporting standards
IROs	Impacts, risks and opportunities
ISSB	International Sustainability Standards Board
NFRD	Non-Financial Reporting Directive
SCGI	Sustainable corporate governance initiative
SR	Sustainability reporting
UK	United Kingdom

References

Aarikka-Stenroos, L., Ritala, P., & Thomas, L. D. (2021). Circular economy ecosystems: A typology, definitions, and implications. In S. Teerikangas, T. Onkila, K. Koistinen, & M. Mäkeläand (Eds.), *Research handbook of sustainability agency* (pp. 260–276).

Abbott, K. W., Levi-Faur, D., & Snidal, D. (2017). Theorizing regulatory intermediaries: The RIT model. *ANNALS of the American Academy of Political and Social Science*, 670(1), 14–35.

Abela, M. (2022). A new direction? The 'mainstreaming' of sustainability reporting. *Sustainability Accounting, Management and Policy Journal*, 13(6), 1261–1283. https://doi.org/10.1108/SAMPJ-06-2021-0201.

Abhayawansa, S. (2022). Swimming against the tide: Back to single materiality for sustainability reporting. *Sustainability Accounting, Management and Policy Journal*, 13(6), 1361–1385.

Adams, C. A., & Abhayawansa, S. (2022). Connecting the COVID-19 pandemic, environmental, social and governance (ESG) investing and calls for 'harmonisation' of sustainability reporting. *Critical Perspectives on Accounting*, 82, 102309.

Adams, C. A., & Mueller, F. (2022). Academics and policymakers at odds: The case of the IFRS Foundation Trustees' consultation paper on sustainability reporting. *Sustainability Accounting, Management and Policy Journal*, 13(6), 1310–1333. https://doi.org/10.1108/SAMPJ-10-2021-0436.

Aglietta, M., & Reberioux, A. (2005). *Corporate governance adrift: A critique of shareholder value*. Edward Elgar.

Ahlström, H., & Monciardini, D. (2022). The regulatory dynamics of sustainable finance: Paradoxical success and limitations of EU reforms. *Journal of Business Ethics*, 177(1), 193–212.

Ali, I., Fukofuka, P. T., & Narayan, A. K. (2023). Critical reflections on sustainability reporting standard setting. *Sustainability Accounting, Management and Policy Journal*, 14(4), 776–791, https://doi.org/10.1108/SAMPJ-01-2022-0054.

Alliance for Corporate Transparency (2020) *2019 Research report. An analysis of the sustainability reports of 1000 companies pursuant to the EU Non-Financial Reporting Directive*. Alliance for Corporate Transparency. https://www.eciia.eu/wp-content/uploads/2022/03/2019_Research_Report-_Alliance_for_Corporate_Transparency-7d9802a0c18c9f13017d686481bd2d6c6886fea6d9e9c7a5c3cfafea8a48b1c7.pdf.

References

Archer, M. (2024). *Unsustainable: Measurement, reporting, and the limits of corporate sustainability*. New York University Press.

Arjaliès, D. L., Rodrigue, M., & Romi, A. M. (2023). 'Come play with us!' A grassroots research agenda for accounting and the circular economy. *Accounting Forum*, 47(4), 497–524. https://doi.org/10.1080/01559982.2023.2269747.

ASSC (1975). *The corporate report*. Accounting Standards Steering Committee.

Baboukardos, D., Gaia, S., Lassou, P., & Soobaroyen, T. (2023, April). The multiverse of non-financial reporting regulation. In *Accounting forum* (Vol. 47, no. 2, pp. 147–165). Routledge.

Bach, V., Lehmann, A., Görmer, M., & Finkbeiner, M. (2018). Product environmental footprint (PEF) pilot phase – comparability over flexibility? *Sustainability*, 10(8), 2898.

Bacq, S., & Aguilera, R. V. (2022). Stakeholder governance for responsible innovation: A theory of value creation, appropriation, and distribution. *Journal of Management Studies*, 59(1), 29–60.

Barker, R. (2025). Corporate sustainability reporting. *Journal of Accounting and Public Policy*, 49, 107280.

Barker, R., & Mayer. C. (2024). Seeing double corporate reporting through the materiality lenses of both investors and nature. *Accounting Forum*, 49(2), 259–289. https://doi.org/10.1080/01559982.2023.2277982.

Barnier, M. (2014). The EU transparency and accounting directives. *Journal of World Energy Law and Business*, 7(1), 16–19.

Bebbington, J., Österblom, H., Crona, B., et al. (2020). Accounting and accountability in the Anthropocene. *Accounting, Auditing & Accountability Journal*, 33(1), 152–177. https://doi.org/10.1108/AAAJ-11-2018-3745.

Bebbington, J., Larrinaga, C., & Michelon, G. (2024). A socio-ecological approach to corporate governance. In *Handbook on corporate governance and corporate social responsibility* (pp. 359–370). Edward Elgar Publishing.

Biondi, L., Dumay, J., & Monciardini, D. (2020). Using the international integrated reporting framework to comply with EU directive 2014/95/EU: Can we afford another reporting façade? *Meditari Accountancy Research*, 28(5), 889–914.

Biondi, Y., & Zambon, S. (Eds.). (2013). *Accounting and business economics: Insights from national traditions*. Routledge.

Birch, K., & Muniesa, F. (Eds.). (2020). *Assetization: Turning things into assets in technoscientific capitalism*. MIT Press.

Bohn, L., Macagnan, C. B., & Kronbauer, C. A. (2025). Navigating legitimacy: Diverse stakeholder perspectives on the IFRS Foundation's establishment of the ISSB. *Meditari Accountancy Research*, 33(1), 86–113.

Bothello, J., & Salles-Djelic, M. -L. (2018). Evolving conceptualizations of organizational environmentalism: A path generation account. *Organization Studies*, 39(1), 93–119. https://doi.org/10.1177/0170840617693272.

Botzem, S. (2012). *The politics of accounting regulation: Organizing transnational standard setting in financial reporting*. Edward Elgar.

Botzem, S., & Quack, S. (2005). Contested rules and shifting boundaries: International standard-setting in accounting. *WZB Discussion Paper*, No. SP III 2005-201.

Bourdieu, P. (1984). *Distinction: A social critique of the judgement of taste*. Harvard University Press.

Bourdieu, P. (1996). *The state nobility: Elite schools in the field of power*. Stanford University Press.

Brand-Correa, L., Brook, A., Büchs, M., et al. (2022). Economics for people and planet – moving beyond the neoclassical paradigm. *The Lancet Planetary Health*, 6(4), e371–e379.

Braun, E. (2025). Christmas for lobbyists, Halloween for NGOs. Politico, 27 February. www.politico.eu/newsletter/politico-eu-influence/christmas-for-lobbyists-halloween-for-ngos/.

Brès, L., Mena, S., & Salles-Djelic, M. L. (2019). Exploring the formal and informal roles of regulatory intermediaries in transnational multistakeholder regulation. *Regulation & Governance*, 13(2), 127–140.

Bromley, P., & Powell, W. W. (2012). From smoke and mirrors to walking the talk: Decoupling in the contemporary world. *Academy of Management Annals*, 6(1), 483–530.

Brown, G., El-Erian, M., Spence, M., & Lidow, R. (2023). *Permacrisis: A plan to fix a fractured world*. Simon and Schuster.

Brown, J., & Dillard, J. (2015). Dialogic accountings for stakeholders: On opening up and closing down participatory governance. *Journal of Management Studies*, 52(7), 961–985.

Brown, G., El-Erian, M., Spence, M., & Lidow, R. (2023). *Permacrisis: A plan to fix a fractured world*. Simon and Schuster.

Brunetti, A., Packroff, J., & Bourgery-Gonse, T. (2024). Europe's largest industry groups to double down on EU rule roll-back agenda. 21 November. Euractive. www.euractiv.com/section/economy-jobs/news/europes-largest-industry-groups-to-double-down-on-eu-rule-roll-back-agenda/.

Bueno, N., Bernaz, N., Holly, G., & Martin-Ortega, O. (2024). The EU directive on corporate sustainability due diligence (CSDDD): The final political compromise. *Business and Human Rights Journal*, 9(2), 294–300.

Buhr, N., Gray, R., & Milne, M. J. (2014). Histories, rationales, voluntary standards and future prospects for sustainability reporting: CSR, GRI, IIRC and beyond. In J. Bebbington, J. Unerman, & B. O'Dwyer (Eds.), *Sustainability accounting and accountability* (2nd ed., pp. 51–71). Routledge.

Buller, A. (2022). *The value of a whale: On the illusions of green capitalism*. Manchester University Press.

Burchell, S., Clubb, C., & Hopwood, A. G. (1980), The roles of accounting in organisations and society. *Accounting, Organizations and Society*, 5(1), 5–27.

Burlaud, A., & Colasse, B. (2011). International accounting standardisation: Is politics back? *Accounting in Europe*, 8(1), 23–47. https://doi.org/10.1080/17449480.2011.574412.

Business Roundtable (2019). Business roundtable redefines the purpose of a corporation to promote 'an economy that serves all Americans'. www.businessroundtable.org/business-roundtable-redefines-the-purpose-of-a-corporation-to-promote-an-economy-that-serves-all-americans.

Callahan, C. W., & Mankin, J. S. (2025). Carbon majors and the scientific case for climate liability. *Nature*, 640(8060), 893–901.

Carlsson-Wall, M., Håkansson, H., Kraus, K., Lind, J., & Strömsten, T. (2018) (Eds). *Accounting, innovation and inter-organisational relationships*. Routledge.

Carney, M. (2021). *Values: Building a better world for all*. Signal.

Carpenter, D., & Moss, D. A. (2014). *Preventing regulatory capture*. Cambridge University Press.

Carruthers, B. G., & Espeland, W. N. (2012). Accounting for rationality: Double-entry bookkeeping and the rhetoric of economic rationality. *American Journal of Sociology*, 97(1), 31–69.

Chapman, C. S., Cooper, D. J., & Miller, P. (Eds.). (2009). *Accounting, organizations, and institutions: Essays in honour of Anthony Hopwood*. Oxford University Press.

Chevalier, A. (1976). *Le Bilan Social de l'Entreprise*. Masson.

Chiapello, E. (2015). Financialisation of valuation. *Human Studies*, 38(1), 13–35.

Chiapello, E. (2016). How IFRS contribute to the financialization of capitalism. In D. Bensadon, N. Praquin (Eds.), *IFRS in a global world* (pp. 71–84). Springer. https://doi.org/10.1007/978-3-319-28225-1_6.

Chiapello, E., & Medjad, K. (2009). An unprecedented privatisation of mandatory standard-setting: The case of European accounting policy. *Critical perspectives on Accounting*, 20(4), 448–468.

Cho, C. H., Laine, M., Roberts, R. W., & Rodrigue, M. (2015a). Organized hypocrisy, organizational façades, and sustainability reporting. *Accounting, Organizations and Society*, 40, 78–94.

Cho, C. H., Michelon, G., & Patten, D. M. (2012). Impression management in sustainability reports: An empirical investigation of the use of graphs. *Accounting and the Public Interest*, 12(1), 16–37.

Cho, C., & Patten, D. M. (2007). The role of environmental disclosure as legitimacy tools: A research note. *Accounting Organizations and Society*, 32(7), 639–647.

Cho, C. H., Michelon, G., Patten, D. M., & Roberts, R. W. (2015b). CSR disclosure: The more things change … ? *Accounting, Auditing & Accountability Journal*, 28(1), 14–35.

Clarke, T. (2024). *International corporate governance*. Routledge.

Cooper, S, & Michelon, G. (2022). Conceptions of materiality in sustainability reporting frameworks: Commonalities, differences and possibilities. In C. Adams (Ed.), *Handbook of Accounting and Sustainability* (pp. 44–66). Edward Elgar.

Cooper, S., & Owen, D. L. (2007). Corporate social reporting and stakeholder accountability: The missing link. *Accounting, Organizations and Society*, 32 (7–8), 649–667.

Crouch, C. (2009). Privatised Keynesianism. An unacknowledged policy regime. *British Journal of Policies and International Relations*, 11(3), 382–399.

Crouch, C. (2011), *The strange non-death of neoliberalism*. Polity Press: Cambridge.

de Bakker, F. G., Matten, D., Spence, L. J., & Wickert, C. (2020). The elephant in the room: The nascent research agenda on corporations, social responsibility, and capitalism. *Business & Society*. https://journals.sagepub.com/doi/full/10.1177/0007650319898196.

De Schutter, O. (2008), Corporate social responsibility European style. *European Law Journal*, 14, 203–236.

de Villiers, C., Dimes, R., La Torre, M., & Molinari, M. (2024), The International Sustainability Standards Board's (ISSB) past, present, and future: Critical reflections and a research agenda. *Pacific Accounting Review*, 36(2), 255–273. https://doi.org/10.1108/PAR-02-2024-0038.

Deegan, C. (2002), Introduction: The legitimising effect of social and environmental disclosures—a theoretical foundation. *Accounting, Auditing and Accountability Journal*, 15(3), 282–311.

Deegan, C., & Rankin, M. (1999). The environmental reporting expectations gap: Australian evidence. *The British Accounting Review*, 31(3), 313–346.

Deloitte and The Economist Intelligence Unit (2004) *In the dark: what boards and executives don't know about the health of their business*. Deloitte.

Deloitte (2024) Sustainability regulation outlook 2024 https://www.deloitte.com/us/en/insights/topics/environmental-social-governance/sustainability-regulation-outlook.html.

Dey, C. (2003). Corporate 'silent' and 'shadow' social accounting. *Social and Environmental Accountability Journal*, 23(2), 6–9.

Dezalay, Y., & Madsen, M. R. (2012). The force of law and lawyers: Pierre Bourdieu and the reflexive sociology of law. *Annual Review of Law and Social Sciences*, 8, 433–452.

Dierkes, M. (1979). Corporate social reporting in Germany: Conceptual developments and practical experience. *Accounting, Organizations and Society*, 4 (1/2), 87–107.

Dillard, J., & Vinnari, E. (2019). Critical dialogical accountability: From accounting-based accountability to accountability-based accounting. *Critical Perspectives on Accounting*, 62, 16–38.

Diouf, D., & Boiral, O. (2017). The quality of sustainability reports and impression management. *Accounting, Auditing & Accountability Journal*, 30(3), 643–667.

Djelic & Sahlin (2009). Governance and its transnational dynamics: Towards a reordering of our world? In C. S. Chapman, D. J. Cooper, & P. Miller (Eds.), *Accounting, organizations, and institutions: Essays in honour of Anthony Hopwood* (175–204). Oxford University Press.

Djelic, M. L., & Etchanchu, H. (2017). Contextualizing corporate political responsibilities: Neoliberal CSR in historical perspective. *Journal of Business Ethics*, *142*(4), 641–661.

Dombrovskis, V. (2025). Remarks by Commissioner Dombrovskis at the press conference presenting Omnibus proposals to simplify EU rules. Press Release 26 February. https://ec.europa.eu/commission/presscorner/detail/en/statement_25_629.

ECB – European Central Bank (2025). Opinion of the European Central Bank of 8 May 2025 on proposals for amendments to corporate sustainability reporting and due diligence requirements (CON/2025/10). www.ecb.europa.eu/pub/pdf/legal/ecb.leg_con_2025_10.en.pdf.

ECCJ – European Coalition for Corporate Justice (2020). Over 100 civil society organisations demand human rights and environmental due diligence legislation. 2 December 2019. https://corporatejustice.org/news/16800-over-100-civil-society-organisations-demand-human-rights-and-environmental-due-diligence-legislation.

ECCJ – European Coalition for Corporate Justice (2025). Omnibus proposal will create costly confusion and lower protection for people and the planet. Joint Statement by over 170 members of civil society, human rights and environmental defenders, trade unions and climate activists. 14 January. https://corporatejustice.org/publications/joint-statement-on-omnibus/.

Eccles, R. G., & Klimenko, S. (2019). The investor revolution. *Harvard Business Review*, 97(3), 106–116.

Edelman, L. B. (2016). *Working law: Courts, corporations, and symbolic civil rights*. University of Chicago Press.

Edgley, C. (2014). A genealogy of accounting materiality. *Critical Perspectives on Accounting*, 25(3), 255–271.

EFRAG and IFRS Foundation (2024). *ESRS-ISSB standards: Interoperability guidance*. www.efrag.org/sites/default/files/sites/webpublishing/SiteAssets/ESRS-ISSB%20Standards%20Interoperability%20Guidance.pdf.

Epstein, G. A. (Ed.). (2005). *Financialization and the world economy*. Edward Elgar.

ERT (2025). Reducing the reporting burden in the EU. European Round Table for Industry.

ESMA (2020). Enforcement and regulatory activities of European enforcers in 2019. April 2020. www.esma.europa.eu/document/enforcement-and-regulatory-activities-european-enforcers-in-2019.

Etzion, D., & Ferraro, F. (2010). The role of analogy in the institutionalization of sustainability reporting. *Organization Science*, 21(5), 1092–1107.

European Commission (2001). *European commission recommendation, 4th and 5th Recitals of the preamble, 2001*. https://eur-lex.europa.eu/legal-content/EN/TXT/HTML/?uri=CELEX:32001H0453&from=ET.

European Commission (2002). *A business contribution to sustainable development*. 347 final of 2.7.2002, Brussels. http://eurlex.europa.eu/LexUriServ/LexUriServ.do?uri=COM:2002:0347:FIN:en:PDF.

European Commission (2009). Regulation (EC) No 1221/2009 on the voluntary participation by organisations in a Community eco-management and audit scheme (EMAS). https://eur-lex.europa.eu/legal-content/EN/TXT/?uri=legissum:ev0022.

European Commission (2013). Impact assessment accompanying the proposal for a directive as regards disclosure of nonfinancial and diversity information by certain large companies and groups. Brussels. 16th April, https://eur-lex.europa.eu/legal-content/EN/TXT/PDF/?uri=CELEX:52013SC0127#:~:text=This%20Impact%20Assessment%20considers%20the,highly%20competitive%20social%20market%20economy.

European Commission (2017a). Frequently asked questions: Guidelines on disclosure of non-financial information. Brussels, 26 June 2017. http://europa.eu/rapid/press-release_MEMO-17-1703_en.htm?locale=en.

European Commission (2017b). Moving towards a circular economy with EMAS. Best practices to implement circular economy strategies (with case study examples). Luxembourg: Publications Office of the European Union.

European Commission (2018). Communication from the commission: Action plan: Financing sustainable growth, COM(2018) 97 final.

European Commission (2019a). Communication from the Commission: Guidelines on non-financial reporting: Supplement on reporting climate-related information (2019/C 209/01), OJ C 209. 20 6.2019, pp. 1–30. https://eur-lex.europa.eu/legal-content/EN/TXT/PDF/?uri=CELEX:52019XC0620(01)&from=EN.

European Commission (2019b). Communication from the Commission: The European Green Deal. 11 December, COM(2019) 649 final.

European Commission (2020). Circular economy action plan: For a cleaner and more competitive Europe. https://ec.europa.eu/environment/circular-economy/pdf/new_circular_economy_action_plan.pdf.

European Commission (2021). Proposal for a directive of the European parliament and of the council amending Directive 2013/34/EU, Directive 2004/109/EC, Directive 2006/43/EC and Regulation (EU) No 537/2014, as regards corporate sustainability reporting. 21.4.2021, COM/2021/189 final.

European Commission (2022). Proposal for a directive of the European parliament and of the council on corporate sustainability due diligence and amending directive (EU) 2019/1937, 23.2.2022, COM(2022) 71 final.

European Commission (2023). Commission delegated regulation (EU) 2023/2772 of 31 July 2023 supplementing Directive 2013/34/EU of the European parliament and of the Council as regards sustainability reporting standards, C/2023/5303, OJ L, 2023/2772, 22.12.2023, ELI: http://data.europa.eu/eli/reg_del/2023/2772/oj.

European Commission (2023b). Delivering today and preparing for tomorrow: The 2024 commission work programme. Press Release, 17 October, https://ec.europa.eu/commission/presscorner/detail/en/ip_23_4965.

European Commission (2025a). An EU compass to regain competitiveness and secure sustainable prosperity. Press Release, 29 January. https://ec.europa.eu/commission/presscorner/detail/en/ip_25_339.

European Commission (2025b). Commission simplifies rules on sustainability and EU investments, delivering over €6 billion in administrative relief. 26 February. https://ec.europa.eu/commission/presscorner/detail/en/ip_25_614.

European Environmental Agency (2024). European climate risk assessment. www.eea.europa.eu/en/analysis/publications/european-climate-risk-assessment.

European Parliament. (2025). Cutting red tape and simplifying business in the EU: The first Omnibus proposals' (debate). European Parliament, 10 March, Strasburg. www.europarl.europa.eu/doceo/document/CRE-10-2025-03-10-ITM-016_EN.html.

European Union (1978). Fourth council directive 78/660/EEC of 25 July 1978 based on Article 54 (3) (g) of the Treaty on the annual accounts of certain types of companies, OJ L 222, 14 8.1978, pp. 11–31.

European Union (1983). Seventh council directive 83/349/EEC of 13 June 1983 based on the Article 54 (3) (g) of the treaty on consolidated accounts, OJ L 193, 18 7.1983, pp. 1–17.

European Union (2002). Regulation (EC) No 1606/2002 of the European parliament and of the council of 19 July 2002 on the application of international accounting standards, OJ L 243, 11 9.2002, pp. 1–4.

European Union (2013). Directive 2013/34/EU of the European parliament and of the council of 26 June 2013 on the annual financial statements, consolidated financial statements and related reports of certain types of undertakings, amending Directive 2006/43/EC of the European parliament and of the council and repealing council directives 78/660/EEC and 83/349/EEC, OJ L 182, 29 6.2013, pp. 19–76.

European Union (2014). Directive 2014/95/EU of the European parliament and of the council of 22 October 2014 amending directive 2013/34/EU as regards disclosure of non-financial and diversity information by certain large undertakings and groups, OJ L 330, 15.11.2014, pp. 1–9.

European Union. (2022). Directive (EU) 2022/2464 of the European parliament and of the Council of 14 December 2022 amending regulation (EU) No 537/2014, directive 2004/109/EC, directive 2006/43/EC and directive 2013/34/EU, as regards corporate sustainability reporting, PE/35/2022/REV/1, OJ L 322, 16.12.2022, pp. 15–80.

European Union (2024) Regulation (EU) 2024/1781 establishing a framework for the setting of ecodesign requirements for sustainable products. 13 June 2024. https://eur-lex.europa.eu/eli/reg/2024/1781/oj.

Faber, E. (2023). Comptabilité d'entreprise : « Exiger que la matérialité s'étende au-delà du domaine économique est en réalité simpliste » Tribune,

Le Monde, 10 October, www.lemonde.fr/idees/article/2023/10/10/comptabi lite-d-entreprise-exiger-que-la-materialite-s-etende-au-dela-du-domaine-economique-est-en-realite-simpliste_6193607_3232.html.

Fairbrass, J. (2011). Exploring corporate social responsibility policy in the European Union: A discursive institutionalist analysis. *JCMS*, 49(5), 949–970.

Fink, L. (2018). *A sense of purpose. Larry Fink's 2018 letter to CEOs*. BlackRock. www.blackrock.com/corporate/investor-relations/2018-larry-fink-ceo-letter.

Fleischman, R. K. (2004). Confronting moral issues from accounting's dark side. *Accounting History*, 9(1), 7–23.

Fligstein, N., & Shin, T.-J. (2004). The shareholder value society: A review of the changes in working conditions and inequality in the United States, 1976 to 2000. *Social Inequality* (pp. 401–432). Russell Sage Foundation.

Flower, J. (2015). The international integrated reporting council: A story of failure. *Critical Perspectives on Accounting*, 27, 1–17.

FoE (2025). NGOs challenge EU Commission's undemocratic omnibus process, Friends of Earth Europe. 18 April. https://friendsoftheearth.eu/press-release/ngos-challenge-eu-commissions-undemocratic-omnibus-process/.

Fransen, L., & LeBaron, G. (2019). Big audit firms as regulatory intermediaries in transnational labor governance. *Regulation & Governance*, 13(2), 260–279.

Friede, G., Busch, T., & Bassen, A. (2015). ESG and financial performance: Aggregated evidence from more than 2000 empirical studies. *Journal of Sustainable Finance & Investment*, 5(4), 210–233. https://doi.org/10.1080/20430795.2015.1118917.

Gazdar, K. (2007). *Reporting nonfinancials*. Wiley.

Giner, B., & Jorissen, A. (2020). Special issue on accounting and politics. *Accounting in Europe*, 17(3), 239–242. https://doi.org/10.1080/17449480.2020.1841905.

Giner, B., & Luque-Vílchez, M. (2022). A commentary on the 'new' institutional actors in sustainability reporting standard-setting: A European perspective'. *Sustainability Accounting, Management and Policy Journal*, 13(6), 1284–1309. https://doi.org/10.1108/SAMPJ-06-2021-0222.

Glaum, M. (2000). Bridging the GAAP: The changing attitude of German managers towards Anglo-American accounting and accounting harmonization. *Journal of International Financial Management & Accounting*, 11(1), 23–47.

Gond, J.-P., & Igalens, J. (2012). *La Responsabilité sociale de l'entreprise*. Puf.

Gourevitch, P. A. and J. Shinn (2005), *Political power and corporate control: The new global politics of corporate governance*. Princeton University Press.

Gramsci, A. (1971). *Selections from the prison notebooks of Antonio Gramsci* (Q. Hoare & G. NowellSmith, Trans.). International.

Gray, R. (2006). Social, environmental and sustainability reporting and organisational value creation? Whose value? Whose creation?. *Accounting, Auditing & Accountability Journal*, 19(6), 793–819. https://doi.org/10.1108/09513570610709872.

Gray, R. (2010). Is accounting for sustainability actually accounting for sustainability ... and how would we know? An exploration of narratives of organisations and the planet. *Accounting, Organizations and Society*, 35(1), 47–62.

Gray, R., Dillar, J., & Spence, C. (2009). Social accounting as if the world matters. *Public Management Review*, 11 (5), 545–573.

Greenwood, M., & Kamoche, K. (2013). Social accounting as stakeholder knowledge appropriation. *Journal of Management & Governance*, 17(3), 723–743.

Groppi, T. (2023). Sustainability and constitutions: Constitutional law and the dilemma of the future. *Wroclaw Review of Law, Administration & Economics*, 13(1), 1–12.

Gros, M. (2025). Brussels confirms dramatic U-turn on corporate green rules. Politico, 26 February. www.politico.eu/article/most-eu-firms-exempted-from-green-reporting-under-proposed-omnibus-bill/.

Guthrie, J., & Parker, L. D. (1989). Corporate social reporting: a rebuttal of legitimacy theory. *Accounting and Business Research*, *19*(76), 343–352.

Hägg, C. (1984). The OECD guidelines for multinational enterprises. *Journal of Business Ethics*, 3(1), 71–76.

Hahn, R., Reimsbach, D., & Wickert, C. (2023). Nonfinancial reporting and real sustainable change: Relationship status – it's complicated. *Organization & Environment*, 36, 3–16.

Haldane, A., Migliavacca, A., & Palea, V. (2024). Is accounting a matter for bookkeepers only? The effects of IFRS adoption on the financialization of economy. *Cambridge Journal of Economics*, 48(3), 489–512.

Hall, N. L., & Jeanneret, T. (2015). Social licence to operate: An opportunity to enhance CSR for deeper communication and engagement. *Corporate Communications: An International Journal*, 20(2), 213–227.

Haller, A. (1992). The relationship of financial and tax accounting in Germany: A major reason for accounting disharmony in Europe. *The International Journal of Accounting*, 27, 310–323.

Haller, A. (2002). Financial accounting developments in the European Union: past events and future prospects. *European Accounting Review*, *11*(1), 153–190

Hardyment, R. (2024). *Measuring good business: Making sense of environmental, social and governance (ESG) data*. Taylor & Francis.

Harribey, L. E. (2009). France. In S. O. Idowu, & W. Leal Filho (Eds.), *Global Practices of Corporate Social Responsibility* (pp. 249–250). Springer-Verlag.

Harvey, D. (2007).*A brief history of neoliberalism*. Oxford University Press.

Hein, E., Detzer, D., & Dodig, N. (2016). *Financialization and the financial and economic crises: Country studies*. Edward Elgar.

Heinelt, H. (2019). *Sustainability, innovation and participatory governance: A cross-national study of the EU eco-management and audit scheme*. Routledge.

Helms, W. S., Oliver, C., & Webb, K. (2012). Antecedents of settlement on a new institutional practice: Negotiation of the ISO 26000 standard on social responsibility. *Academy of Management Journal*, 55(5), 1120–1145.

Herlin-Karnell, E. (2023). The constitutional concepts of sustainability and dignity. *Jus Cogens*, 5(2), 125–148.

Hesse, M. B. (1963). *Models and analogies in Science*. Sheed & Ward.

Hoffman, A. (2023). Why management research needs a radical rethink. *Financial Times*. www.ft.com/content/0500d456-6c2d-4bc9-af85-e4be5c9ae5d1.

Hoogervorst, H., & Prada, M. (2015). *Working in the public interest: The IFRS Foundation and the IASB*. IFRS Foundation, 1–12.

Hopwood, A. G. (1983), On trying to study accounting in the context in which it operates. *Accounting, Organizations and Society*, 8(2–3), 287–305.

Hopwood, A. G. (1992). Accounting calculation and the shifting sphere of the economic. *European Accounting Review*, 1(1), 125–143.

Hopwood, A. (1994). Some reflections on the harmonization of accounting in the EU. *European Accounting Review*, 3(2), 241–253.

Hopwood, A. G., & Miller, P. (Eds.). (1994). *Accounting as social and institutional practice* (Vol. 24). Cambridge University Press.

Hopwood, A. G. (2007). Whither accounting research? *The Accounting Review*, 82(5), 1365–1374.

Horn, L. (2011). *Regulating corporate governance in the EU – Towards a marketisation of corporate control*, Palgrave.

Howarth, D. (2005). Applying discourse theory: The method of articulation. In D. Howarth & J. Torfing (Eds.), *Discourse theory in European politics: Identity, policy and governance* (pp. 316–349). Palgrave Macmillan.

Hummel, K., & Jobst, D. (2024). An overview of corporate sustainability reporting legislation in the European Union. *Accounting in Europe*, 21(3), 320–355.

IDVO (2025). Broad support for the CSDDD. www.we-support-the-csddd.eu/.

IFAG (2025). The state of play: Sustainability disclosure and assurance. Five year trends and analysis 2019–2023. IFAG. www.ifac.org/knowledge-gateway/audit-assurance/publications/state-play-sustainability-disclosure-and-assurance.

IIRC (2011). Towards integrated reporting, communicating value in the 21st century. https://integratedreporting.ifrs.org/wp-content/uploads/2011/09/IR-Discussion-Paper-2011_spreads.pdf.

IOSCO (2023). IOSCO endorses the ISSB's sustainability-related financial disclosures standards, 25th July, Madrid Media Release. www.iosco.org/news/pdf/IOSCONEWS703.pdf.

IPCC. (2023). Climate change 2023: Synthesis report. Contribution of working groups I, II and III to the sixth assessment report of the intergovernmental panel on climate change (Core Writing Team, H. Lee and J. Romero (Eds.)). IPCC, Geneva, Switzerland, p.184. https://doi10.59327/IPCC/AR6-9789291691647.

Iraldo, F., & Barberio, M. (2017). Drivers, barriers and benefits of the EU Ecolabel in European companies' perception. *Sustainability*, 9(5), 751–766.

Iraldo, F., Testa, F., & Frey, M. (2009). Is an environmental management system able to influence environmental and competitive performance? The case of the eco-management and audit scheme (EMAS) in the European union. *Journal of Cleaner Production*, 17(16), 1444–1452.

Ireland, P., & Pillay, R. G. (2010). Corporate social responsibility in a neoliberal age. In P. Utting, & J. C. Marques (Eds.), *Corporate social responsibility and regulatory governance* (pp. 77–104). Palgrave Macmillan.

Jackson, T. (2009) *Prosperity without growth: Economics for a finite planet*. Routledge.

Jessop, B. (1992). Fordism and post-Fordism: A critical reformulation. In M. Storper, A. J. Scott (Eds.), *Pathways to industrialization and regional development* (pp. 42–62). Routledge.

Jessop, B. (2007). Regulation- and state-theoretical perspectives on changes in corporate governance and metagovernance. In H. Overbeek, B. Van Apeldoorn, & A. Nolke (Eds.), *The transnational politics of corporate governance regulation* (pp. 65–80). Routledge.

Kallis, G., Hickel, J., O'Neill, D. W., et al. (2025). Post-growth: The science of wellbeing within planetary boundaries. *The Lancet Planetary Health*, 9(1), e62–e78.

Kampourakis, I. (2018). CSR and social rights: Juxtaposing societal constitutionalism and rights-based approaches imposing human rights obligations on corporations. *Goettingen Journal of International Law*, 9, 537–569.

Khaitan, T. (2019). Constitutional directives: Morally-committed political constitutionalism. *The Modern Law Review*, 82(4), 603–632.

Kinderman, D. (2012). 'Free us up so we can be responsible!' The co-evolution of corporate social responsibility and neo-liberalism in the UK, 1977–2010. *Socio-Economic Review*, 10(1), 29–57.

Kinderman, D. (2013). Corporate social responsibility in the EU, 1993–2013: Institutional ambiguity, economic crises, business legitimacy and bureaucratic politics. *JCMS: Journal of Common Market Studies*, 51(4), 701–720.

Kinderman, D. (2016). Time for a reality check: Is business willing to support a smart mix of complementary regulation in private governance? *Policy and Society*, 35(1), 29–42.

Kinderman, D. (2019). The challenges of upward regulatory harmonization: The case of sustainability reporting in the European Union. *Regulation & Governance*. https://doi.org/10.1111/rego.12240.

Klamer, A., & McCloskey, D. (1992). Accounting as the master metaphor of economics. *European Accounting Review*, 1(1), 145–160.

Klettner, A., Clarke, T., & Boersma, M. (2014). The governance of corporate sustainability: Empirical insights into the development, leadership and implementation of responsible business strategy. *Journal of Business Ethics*, 122, 145–165. https://doi.org/10.1007/s10551-013-1750-y.

Knudsen, J. S., & Moon, J. (2017). *Visible hands: Government regulation and international business responsibility*. Cambridge University Press.

Knudsen, J. S., & Moon, J. (2022). Corporate social responsibility and government: The role of discretion for engagement with public policy. *Business Ethics Quarterly*, 32, 243–271.

Knudsen, J. S., Moon, J., & Slager, R. (2015). Government policies for corporate social responsibility in Europe: A comparative analysis of institutionalisation. *Policy & Politics*, 43(1), 81–99.

Koch, M. (2011). *Capitalism and climate change: Theoretical discussion, historical development and policy responses*. Palgrave Macmillan.

Koenig-Archibugi, M., & Macdonald, K. (2017). The role of beneficiaries in transnational regulatory processes. *ANNALS of the American Academy of Political and Social Science*, 670(1), 36–57.

Kourula, A., Moon, J., Salles-Djelic, M.-L., & Wickert, C. (2019). New roles of government in the governance of business conduct: Implications for management and organizational research. *Organization Studies*, 40(8), 1101–1123. https://doi.org/10.1177/0170840619852142.

La Torre, M., Sabelfeld, S., Blomkvist, M., Tarquinio, L., & Dumay, J. (2018). Harmonising non-financial reporting regulation in Europe: Practical forces and projections for future research. *Meditari Accountancy Research*, 26(4), 598–621.

Laine, M., Tregidga, H., & Unerman, J. (2022). *Sustainability accounting and accountability*. Routledge.

Lawrence, T. B., Hardy, C., & Phillips, N. (2002). Institutional effects of interorganizational collaboration: The emergence of protoinstitutions. *Academy of Management Journal*, 45(1), 281–290.

Lazonick, W. (2023). *Investing in innovation: Confronting predatory value extraction in the US corporation*. Cambridge University Press.

Lazonick, W., & Shin, J. S. (2019). *Predatory value extraction: How the looting of the business enterprise became the US norm and how sustainable prosperity can be restored*. Oxford University Press.

Leali, G., de Likllepin, P., & Fernyhough (2025). Macron and Merz call to abolish EU law on ethical supply chains. Politico. www.politico.eu/article/macron-merz-supply-chain-green-ethical/.

LeBaron, G., Lister, J., & Dauvergne, P. (2017). Governing global supply chain sustainability through the ethical audit regime. *Globalizations*, 14(6), 958–975.

Leinaweaver, J. (2015). Is corporate sustainability reporting a great waste of time? The Guardian, 6 June. www.theguardian.com/sustainable-business/2015/jan/06/corporate-sustainability-reporting-waste-time.

Lenton, T. M., Rockström, J., Gaffney, O., et al. (2019). Climate tipping points – too risky to bet against. *Nature*, 575(7784), 592–595.

Levy, D. L., Brown, H. S. & de Jong, M. (2010). The contested politics of corporate governance. The case of the Global Reporting Initiative. *Business & Society*, 49(1): 88–115.

Lyle, J. T. (1996). *Regenerative design for sustainable development*. John Wiley & Sons.

Maclean, C., & Crouch, C. (2011). Introduction: The economics, political, and ethical challenges of corporate social responsibility. In C. Crouch, & C. Maclean (Eds.), *The responsible corporation in a global economy* (pp. 1–28). Oxford University Press.

Maclean, C., & Crouch, C. (2012). *The responsible corporation*. Oxford University Press.

Madsen M. R. (2006). Transnational fields: Elements of a reflexive sociology of the internationalisation of law. *Retfaerd*, 3(114), 23–41.

Madsen M. R., & Dezalay, Y. (2002). The power of the legal field: Pierre Bourdieu and the law. In R. Banakan, & M. Travars (Eds.), *An introduction to law and social theory* (pp. 189–204). Hart.

Maechler, S. (2023). Accounting for whom? The financialisation of the environmental economic transition. *New Political Economy*, 28(3), 416-432.

Magnan, M. L. (2009). Fair value accounting and the financial crisis: Messenger or contributor? *Accounting Perspectives*, 8(3), 189–213. https://doi.org/10.1506/ap.8.3.1.

Magnan, M., & Michelon, G. (Eds.). (2024). *Handbook on corporate governance and corporate social responsibility*. Edward Elgar, p. 428.

Mähönen, J. (2020). Comprehensive approach to relevant and reliable reporting in Europe: A dream impossible? *Sustainability*, 12, 5277.

Mähönen, J., & Palea, V. (2024). Analyzing double materiality through the lens of the European political constitution: Implications for interoperability and standards-setting. 19 February. University of Oslo Faculty of Law Research Paper No. 2024-05, Nordic & European Company Law Working Paper No. 24,03, https://ssrn.com/abstract=4731089.

Maher, R., Monciardini, D., & Böhm, S. (2020). Torn between legal claiming and privatized remedy: Rights mobilization against gold mining in Chile. *Business Ethics Quarterly*, 31, 37–74.

Marens, R. (2012). Generous in victory? American managerial autonomy, labour relations and the invention of Corporate Social Responsibility. *Socio-Economic Review*, 10 (1), 59–84.

Mathews, M. R. (1997). Twenty-five years of social and environmental accounting research: Is there a silver jubilee to celebrate? *Accounting, Auditing & Accountability Journal*, 10(4), 481–531.

Matten, D., & Crane, A. (2005). Corporate citizenship: Toward an extended theoretical conceptualization. *The Academy of Management Review*, 30(1), 166–179.

Mazzucato, M. (2018). *The value of everything: Making and taking in the global economy*. Hachette UK.

McBarnet, D., Voiculescu, A., & Campbell, T. (2007). *The new corporate accountability: Corporate social responsibility and the law*. Cambridge University Press.

McPhail, K., Macdonald, K., & Ferguson, J. (2016). Should the international accounting standards board have responsibility for human rights? *Accounting, Auditing & Accountability Journal*, 29(4), 594–616. https://doi.org/10.1108/AAAJ-03-2016-2442.

Meadows, D. H., Meadows, D. L., Randers, J., & Behrens III, W. W. (1972). *The limits to growth*. Club of Rome.

Mélon, L. (2026). The EU Non-Financial Reporting Directive and the corporate narrative disclosure practices In T. Clarke, S. Benn, M. Edwards (Eds.), *Routledge Companion to Corporate Sustainability*, Routledge (Chapter 16) https://www.routledge.com/Routledge-Companion-to-Corporate-Sustainability/

Clarke-Benn-Edwards/p/book/9780367509057?srsltid=AfmBOooCGw6xHjnp
NRBlWyexj8bLvsRYcfVLBtuCLtwhbheDrvQCTZRK.

Mennicken, A., & Power, M. (2015). Accounting and the plasticity of valuation. In A. B. Antal, M. Hutter, & S. Stark (Eds.), *Moments of valuation: Exploring sites of dissonance*. Oxford University Press. https://doi.org/10.1093/acprof:oso/9780198702504.003.0011.

Michelon, G., Trojanowski, G., & Sealy, R. (2022). Narrative reporting: State of the art and future challenges. *Accounting in Europe*, 19(1), 7–47, https://doi.org/10.1080/17449480.2021.1900582.

Miller, P. (1998). The margins of accounting. *The Sociological Review*, 46, 174–193. https://doi.org/10.1111/j.1467-954X.1998.tb03474.x.

Miller, P., & Power, M. (2013). Accounting, organizing, and economizing: Connecting accounting research and organization theory. *Academy of Management Annals*, 7(1), 557–605.

Miller, P., & Rose, N. (1990). Governing economic life. *Economy and Society*, 19(1), 1–31.

Milne, M. J., & Gray, R. (2013). W (h) ither ecology? The triple bottom line, the global reporting initiative, and corporate sustainability reporting. *Journal of Business Ethics*, 118, 13–29.

Monciardini, D. (2013). Quello che conta. A Socio-Legal Analysis of Accounting for Sustainable Companies.

Monciardini, D. (2016). The 'coalition of the unlikely' driving the EU regulatory process of non-financial reporting. *Social and Environmental Accountability Journal*, 36(1), 76–89.

Monciardini, D. (2019). *Conflicts and coalitions: The drivers of European corporate sustainability reforms*. Cambridge University Press.

Monciardini, D., & Conaldi, G. (2019). The European regulation of corporate social responsibility: The role of beneficiaries' intermediaries. *Regulation & Governance*, 13(2), 240–259.

Monciardini, D., & Mähönen, J. (2026). Redefining value creation: paradigm changes in corporate reporting. In T. Clarke, S. Benn, & M. Edwards (Eds.), *Routledge companion to corporate sustainability*. Routledge (Chapter 11) https://www.routledge.com/Routledge-Companion-to-Corporate-Sustainability/Clarke-Benn-Edwards/p/book/9780367509057?srsltid=AfmBOooCGw6xHjnp NRBlWyexj8bLvsRYcfVLBtuCLtwhbheDrvQCTZRK.

Monciardini, D., Bernaz, N., & Andhov, A. (2021). The organizational dynamics of compliance with the UK modern slavery act in the food and tobacco sector. *Business & Society*, 60(2), 288–340.

Monciardini, D., Mähönen, J., & Tsagas, G. (2020). Rethinking non-financial reporting: A blueprint for structural regulatory changes. *Accounting,*

Economics, and Law: A Convivium, 10(2), 20200092–20200132. https://doi.org/10.1515/ael-2020-0092.

Monciardini, D., Rocca, L., & Veneziani, M. (2024). Virtuous circles: Transformative impact and challenges of the social and solidarity circular economy. *Business Strategy and the Environment*, 33(2), 642–660.

Moon J. (2004). *Government as a driver of corporate social responsibility: The UK in comparative perspective* (ICCSR Research Paper Series No. 20-2004). Nottingham University Business School.

Morgan, G. (1986). *Images of organization*, Sage.

Müller, J. (2014). An accounting revolution? The financialisation of standard setting. *Critical Perspectives on Accounting*, 25(7), 539–557.

Mundy, S. (2025). EU struggles to balance its green and growth goals. *Financial Times*. www.ft.com/content/6f74926a-6ab3-46ee-a434-573c588b7ff4.

Nobes, C., & Parker, R. H. (2008). *Comparative international accounting*. Pearson Education.

Ocean Tomo (2020). Intangible asset market value study. Ocean Tomo. https://oceantomo.com/insights/ocean-tomo-releases-intangible-asset-market-value-study-interim-results-for-2020/.

OECD (2023), *G20/OECD principles of corporate governance 2023*. OECD Publishing. https://doi.org/10.1787/ed750b30-en.

Overbeek, H., van Apeldoorn, B., & Nölke, A. (Eds.). (2007). *The transnational politics of corporate governance regulation* (Vol. 23). Routledge.

Owen, D. (2008). Chronicles of wasted time? A personal reflection on the current state of, and future prospects for social and environmental accounting research. *Accounting, Auditing and Accountability Journal*, 21(2), 240–267.

Owen, D. L., Swift, T. A., Humphrey, C., & Bower-man, M. C. (2000). The new social audits: Account-ability, managerial capture or the agenda of socialchampions? *European Accounting Review*, 9(1), 81–98.

Pagano, M., & Volpin, P. F. (2005). The political economy of corporate governance. *American Economic Review*, 95(4), 1005–1030.

Palea, V. (2018). Financial reporting for sustainable development: Critical insights into IFRS implementation in the European Union. *Accounting Forum*, 42(3), 248–260. https://doi.org/10.1016/j.accfor.2018.08.001.

Palea, V. (2022). Accounting for sustainable finance: Does fair value measurement fit for long-term equity investments? *Meditari Accountancy Research*, 30(1), 22–38. https://doi.org/10.1108/MEDAR-07-20200965.

Parkinson, J. E. (1996). *Corporate power and responsibility*. Clarendon Press.

Parkinson, J. (2006). Corporate governance and the regulation of business behaviour. In: S. MacLeod (Ed.), *Global governance and the quest for justice. Corporate governance*. Hart Publishing.

Parrique, T. (2025). *Slow down or die*. The Economics of Degrowth. Europa Editions.

Perry, J., & Nölke, A. (2006). The political economy of international accounting standards. *Review of International Political Economy*, 13(4), 559–586.

Plantin, G., Sapra, H., & Shin, H. S. (2008). Marking-to-market: Panacea or Pandora's Box? *Journal of Accounting Research*, 46(2), 435–460. Scopus. https://doi.org/10.1111/j.1475-679X.2008.00281.x.

Polanyi, K. (1944). *The great transformation: The political and economic origins of our time*. Beacon Press.

PwC (2024). *Global CSRD survey 2024*. www.pwc.com/gx/en/issues/esg/global-csrd-survey.html.

Raith, D. (2023). The contest for materiality: What counts as CSR?. *Journal of Applied Accounting Research*, 24(1), 134–148. https://doi.org/10.1108/JAAR-04-2022-0093.

Ramanna, K. (2015). *Political standards: Corporate interest, ideology, and leadership in the shaping of accounting rules for the market economy*. University of Chicago Press.

Rasche, A., & Kell, G. (2025). Sustainability 'post-omnibus' – In search of a new narrative. 28 February. www.linkedin.com/pulse/sustainability-post-omnibus-search-new-narrative-andreas-rasche-8y0tf.

Raworth, K. (2017). *Doughnut economics: Seven ways to think like a 21st century economist*. Penguin Random House, London.

ReclaimFinance (2025). EU Omnibus: A playground for industry lobbies. 6 March. https://reclaimfinance.org/site/en/2025/03/06/eu-omnibus-a-playground-for-industry-lobbies/.

Russell, P., & Dewing, I. (2007). The role of private actors in global governance and regulation: US, European and international convergence of accounting and auditing standards in a post-Enron world. In H. Overbeek, A. Nölke, & B. van Apeldoorn (Eds.), *The transnational politics of corporate governance regulation*. Routledge.

Sapiro, U. (2025). Frankly speaking podcast No 72. *Inside the first wave – A practitioner's perspective on EU reporting*. https://en.frankbold.org/frankly-speaking-podcast/72-ulrike-sapiro-inside-the-first-wave–a-practitioners-perspective-on-eu-reporting.

Scharpf, F. W. (1997). Economic integration, democracy and the welfare state. *Journal of European Public Policy*, 4(1), 18–36.

Scharpf, F. (1999). *Governing in Europe: Effective and democratic?* Oxford University Press.

Scherer, A. G., & Palazzo, G. (2008). Globalization and corporate social responsibility. In A. Crane, A. McWilliams, D. Matten, J. Moon, &

D. Siegel (Eds.), *The Oxford handbook of corporate social responsibility* (pp. 413–431). Oxford University Press.

Scherer, A. G., & Palazzo G. (2011). The new political role of business in a globalized world: A review of a new perspective on CSR and its implications for the firm, governance, and democracy. *Journal of Management Studies*, 48, 899–931.

Scholten, R., Lambooy, T., Renes, R., & Bartels, W. (2020). The impact of climate change in the valuation of production assets via the IFRS framework – An exploratory qualitative comparative case study approach. *Accounting, Economics, and Law: A Convivium*, 10(2), 20180032. https://doi.org/10.1515/ael-2018-0032.

Shift (2023). *Double materiality: What you need to know.* https://shiftproject.org/wp-content/uploads/2023/08/Double-materiality-what-you-need-to-know.pdf.

Shift (2025). https://shiftproject.org/the-european-commissions-omnibus-simplification-proposal-shifts-preliminary-reflections/.

Shipman, A. (2015). *Capitalism without capital: Accounting for the crash.* Springer.

Sikka, P. (2015). The hand of accounting and accountancy firms in deepening income and wealth inequalities and the economic crisis: Some evidence. *Critical Perspectives on Accounting*, 30, 46–62. https://doi.org/10.1016/j.cpa.2013.02.003.

Sjåfjell, B. (2024). Conceptualising corporate sustainability law. 10 December. University of Oslo Faculty of Law Research Paper 2024-13, Nordic & European Company Law Working Paper 25-01, https://ssrn.com/abstract=4865659.

Sjåfjell, B., & Bruner, C. (Eds.). (2019). *The cambridge handbook of corporate law, corporate governance and sustainability.* Cambridge University Press.

Sjåfjell, B. & Wiesbrock, A. (Eds.). (2015). The greening of European business under EU law: Taking article 11 TFEU seriously. Routledge.

Solomon, J. F., Solomon, A., Joseph, N. L., & Norton, S. D. (2013). Impression management, myth creation and fabrication in private social and environmental reporting: Insights from Erving Goffman. *Accounting, Organizations and Society*, 38(3), 195–213.

Sombart, W. (1953). Medioeval and modern commercial enterprise. In F. C. Lane, & J. Riemersma (Eds.), *Enterprise and secular change* (pp. 25–40). Homewood.

Spofforth, M. (2012). View from the top. Mark Spofforth on the value of integrated reporting, in Economia, December, p. 18 http://viewer.zmags.com/publication/cd32abfc#/cd32abfc/18.

Stiglitz, J., Fitoussi, J., & M. Durand, M. (2018). Beyond GDP: Measuring what counts for economic and social performance, OECD, Paris, https://doi.org/10.1787/9789264307292-en.

Stout, L. A. (2012). *The shareholder value myth: How putting shareholders first harms investors, corporations, and the public.* Berrett-Koehler.

Stolowy, H., & Paugam, L. (2023). Sustainability reporting: Is convergence possible? *Accounting in Europe, 20*(2), 139–165.

Strange, S. (1996). *The retreat of the state: The diffusion of power in the world economy.* Cambridge University Press.

Strange, S. (2015). *Casino capitalism.* Manchester University Press.

Streeck, W. (2011). 'The crises of democratic capitalism' in New Left Review No. 71.

Streeck, W. (2014) A Buying Time: The Delayed Crisis of Democratic Capitalism. London: Verso.

Thorell, P., & Whittington, G. (1994). The harmonization of accounting within the EU. Problems, perspectives and strategies. *The European Accounting Review,* 3(2), 215–239.

Tilsted, J. P., Palm, E., Bjørn, A., & Lund, J. F. (2023). Corporate climate futures in the making: Why we need research on the politics of Science-Based Targets. *Energy Research & Social Science,* 103, 103229.

Tinker, A. M. (1980). Towards a political economy of accounting: An empirical illustration of the Cambridge controversies. *Accounting, Organizations and Society,* 5(1), 147–160.

Ullmann, A. A. (1979). Corporate social reporting. *Political Interests and Conflicts in Germany, Accounting, Organizations and Society,* 4, 123–133.

Unerman, J., Bebbington, J., & O'dwyer, B. (Eds.). (2007). *Sustainability accounting and Accountability.* Routledge.

Unerman, J., Bebbington, J., & O'dwyer, B. (2018). Corporate reporting and accounting for externalities. *Accounting and Business Research,* 48(5), 497–522.

Ungericht, B., & Hirt, C. (2010), CSR as a political arena: The struggle for a European framework. *Business and Politics,* 12(4), 1–22.

UNPRI, IIGCC, Eurosif (2025). Investor joint statement on Omnibus legislation. www.unpri.org/download?ac=22691.

Verney, P., & Holmstedt Pell, E. (2023). 'Hell on earth': Inside EFRAG's sustainability standards development drive. Responsible-investor. www.responsible-investor.com/hell-on-earth-how-efforts-to-develop-eus-sustainability-standards-were-marred-by-poor-governance-and-working-conditions/.

Vollmer, H. (2024). Accounting and the shifting spheres: The economic, the public, the planet. *Accounting, Organizations and Society,* 113, 101574.

Wagenhofer, A. (2024). Sustainability reporting: A financial reporting perspective. *Accounting in Europe*, 21(1), 1–13.

WAE and HEC (2025). *2025 post-Omnibus CSRD business survey.* www.weareeurope.group/2025-post-omnibus-csrd-business-survey.

Weber, M. (1927). (reprinted 1981). General economic history. Translated by Frank Knight. New Wedderburn, K. W. (1956). Company law reform. Fabian Society.

Wijen, F. (2014). Means versus ends in opaque institutional fields: Trading off compliance and achievement in sustainability standard adoption. *Academy of Management Review*, 39(3), 302–323.

Williamson, O. E. (1981). The economics of organizations: The transaction cost approach. *American Journal of Sociology* 87(3), 548–577.

Williamson, O. E. (1985). *The eonomic institutions of capitalism.* Free Press.

WWF (2025). Simplification Omnibus: A ticking time bomb for crucial EU sustainable finance laws. 24 February. www.wwf.eu/?17157941/Simplification-Omnibus-A-ticking-time-bomb-for-crucial-EU-sustainable-finance-laws.

Yan, S., Ferraro, F., & Almandoz, J. (2019). The rise of socially responsible investment funds: The paradoxical role of the financial logic. *Administrative Science Quarterly*, 64(2), 466–501.

Zambon, S. (2002). *Locating accounting in its national context: The case of Italy* (Vol. 194). FrancoAngeli.

Acknowledgements

I am grateful to Thomas Clarke for his support and constant encouragement throughout the compilation of this contribution. I would also like to thank many colleagues that inspired this Element. Only to cite a few, Vera Palea, Steffen Böhm, Nadia Bernaz, Beate Sjåfjell, Jukka Mähönen, Stefano Zambon, Yuri Biondi, and Sebastian Botzem.

To the Wild Seas of Cornwall
and the Imposing Mountains of Turin

Cambridge Elements™

Corporate Governance

Thomas Clarke
UTS Business School, University of Technology Sydney

Thomas Clarke is Professor of Corporate Governance at the UTS Business School of the University of Technology Sydney. His work focuses on the institutional diversity of corporate governance and his most recent book is *International Corporate Governance* (Second Edition 2017). He is interested in questions about the purposes of the corporation, and the convergence of the concerns of corporate governance and corporate sustainability.

About the Series

The series Elements in Corporate Governance focuses on the significant emerging field of corporate governance. Authoritative, lively and compelling analyses include expert surveys of the foundations of the discipline, original insights into controversial debates, frontier developments, and masterclasses on key issues. Its areas of interest include empirical studies of corporate governance in practice, regional institutional diversity, emerging fields, key problems and core theoretical perspectives.

Cambridge Elements

Corporate Governance

Elements in the Series

Asian Corporate Governance: Trends and Challenges
Toru Yoshikawa

Value-Creating Boards: Challenges for Future Practice and Research
Morten Huse

Trust, Accountability and Purpose: The Regulation of Corporate Governance
Justin O'Brien

Corporate Governance and Leadership: The Board as the Nexus of Leadership-in-overnance
Monique Cikaliuk, Ljiljana Eraković, Brad Jackson, Chris Noonan and Susan Watson

The Evolution of Corporate Governance
Bob Tricker

Corporate Governance: A Survey
Thomas Clarke

Board Dynamics
Philip Stiles

The Role of the Board in Corporate Purpose and Strategy
Robert Bood, Hans van Ees and Theo Postma

Investing in Innovation: Confronting Predatory Value Extraction in the U.S. Corporation
William Lazonick

The Rhetoric and Reality of Shareholder Democracy and Hedge-Fund Activism
Jan-Sup Shin

Incorporating Purpose: The New Legal Foundations for the Corporation and Its Management
Blanche Segrestin, Kevin Levillain and Armand Hatchuel

Regulating EU Sustainability Reporting: Learning from Failure and Success
David Monciardini

A full series listing is available at: www.cambridge.org/ECG

For EU product safety concerns, contact us at Calle de José Abascal, 56–1°, 28003 Madrid, Spain or eugpsr@cambridge.org.